Murders of Hollywood

Laura Fona

Published by Trellis Publishing, 2021.

MURDERS OF HOLLYWOOD

First edition. July 5, 2021.

Copyright © 2021 Laura Fona.

ISBN: 979-8224063789

Written by Laura Fona.

MURDERS OF HOLLYWOOD

EDITED BY LAURA FONA

THE MURDER OF SAL MINEO

MURDERS OF HOLLYWOOD

AMY DUNCAN

Sal Mineo

"Being in the same room with him and looking at him, I realized that one day I would be in the same position as he, facing death. Before it happens I mean to do the things I want to do. I will not end up saying, "I wish I had".[1]

When Sal Mineo said those words about his dying father, nobody could have predicted that just four short years later, he would, himself, be facing death.[2]

Salvatore and Josephine

Salvatore Mineo Sr moved to America from Sicily in 1929, when he was just 16 years old. He had a strong work ethic and took on any job he could get to earn money, mostly manual labor. He could turn his hand to most things, and worked as an apprentice of sorts to carpenters and builders alike, sawing wood and laying bricks. To supplement his income he also sold small animal figurines, which he would carve out of wood or ivory.

It didn't take the young Sicilian long to find love in the Big Apple, and he set his sights on Josephine Alvisi - an American-born Italian girl who wouldn't even entertain the idea of dating Salvatore until he could speak English. So he learned, amazing Josephine with the speed with which he had picked up the language.

Josephine was impressed with her young suitor's determination and felt it boded well for the future. So much so, in fact, that the couple married at the age of just 18, in 1931.

By the time their first child, Victor, was born in 1935, Salvatore had a steady job working as a cabinet maker. Two years later Josephine gave birth to Michael. According to Sicilian custom, a third son is named after his father so when, on January 10th, 1939, another baby boy was born to the couple, he was named Salvatore.

The family home was a Harlem apartment, but when, shortly after Salvatore's birth, a murder took place outside the building, Josephine and Salvatore Sr. moved their family to a fourth-floor apartment in the Bronx.

By the time Salvatore Jr. came along, his father was working as a casket maker for the Bronx Casket Company. The determination which had so impressed Josephine in the beginning continued, and Salvatore Sr. worked hard, sometimes late into the night to provide for his family. Josephine would tell him that he should be working for himself instead of for someone else, and after their fourth child, Sarina, was born three years after Sal, the family started to seriously think about setting up in business for themselves.

The couple had no money – it was hard scraping by on Salvatore's wage, but friends and family gave him the collateral he needed, and in 1946 the Universal Casket Company was born.

Sal's Early Years

The basement of the building which held the Mineo's apartment was home, in the beginning, to the company. It was slow work – Salvatore Sr. was a meticulous worker and would turn out one or two caskets a week. While her husband was the craftsman of the business, it was Josephine who was the driving force. She saved hard and when she had managed to collect $160 (around $2000 today[3]) she enrolled on a course in business studies. Not only did she take over the bookkeeping of the business, but the ambitious young mother and wife also undertook the securing of orders so that her husband could concentrate on making the caskets.

Although the business premises were in the same building as the apartment, it was a struggle with four young children. Left to their own devices while both their parents worked downstairs the siblings would get into all kinds of mischief – playing on fire escapes, on the street, and even filling balloons with urine and dropping them from the roof.

As each boy grew, he was introduced to the family business, doing whatever he could to help.

Sal, being the youngest boy, was often called upon to look after his baby sister, some days his parents would work from dawn to dusk, and Sal took on their role, feeding her, playing with her, and reading her bedtime stories.

When the young Sal did get to play outside, the other kids would tease him about his father's occupation, and Sal soon learned to stand up for himself – a trait which would land him in trouble again and again.

School

Josephine and Salvatore were staunch Catholics, and when Sal was of school age he, along with his brothers, enrolled in the local church school, St Mary's, which was in the Bronx.

Sal was a small lad and made an easy target for the school bullies. Despite his size, however, he never backed down from a fight and in the fourth grade, he was expelled. His time at St Mary's, though, had given Sal his first taste of performing when the sisters chose him to play the part of a young Jesus.

Josephine managed to enrol Sal in another parochial school, the Holy Family. The transfer hadn't dampened Sal's spirit, however, and his days at the school were few when he was again expelled for fighting.

During that time the business had started to pay dividends. Some of the Mineo's debt had been paid off and there was a small but steady profit coming in. The Mineos felt that being in such an urban environment was bad for the family, so they moved to a house in a different area of the Bronx with fields and open spaces instead of streets and fire escapes. The house was a run down three storey building, and, to help them pay the mortgage, the family moved into the top two floors and rented out the bottom one.

Life was better for the family. The children all had their own rooms, and Josephine had an office in the house to work from.

However, school life had still not improved for Sal. His new school, PS 72, saw him once again picked on because of his size, although this time the young lad managed to assert himself among his peers. When another boy pulled a knife on Sal, he managed to disarm him – and it was probably this victory which started to turn his fortunes around at school.

Acting

Sal was something of a paradox – the tough, smart, street-wise kid who was known for being handy with his fists also loved musicals, a fact which earned him the label of 'sissy' by the neighbourhood kids.

In the summer of 1948, Sal was playing on the street as usual, when a man approached him and his sister, Sarina. He told Sal that he could get him on TV. The other kids laughed, but despite his misgivings, Sal and Sarina brought the man to meet Josephine, who listened cautiously as the stranger told her that her son had talent, and with his looks, he could be on the small screen. There was a dance school in Manhattan, he told her, which could take one more student and he was convinced Sal was the perfect candidate. At the time there was a show called *The Children's Hour* and the man was confident he could get Sal an audition.

Josephine, still suspicious but worn down by Sal's excited chatter and begging, took the man's business card and promised to discuss it with Sal's father.

Despite her misgivings, Josephine decided that dancing might just be the thing to keep Sal off the streets and out of trouble, and it was decided that both he and Sarina would take dance class, while Victor and Mike took music.

The school proved Josephine's suspicions correct, but despite the enrolment fee and the high charge for his portfolio, she carried on with the enrolment, justifying the expense by keeping Sal occupied and out of trouble.

Sal supplemented his family's income by selling newspapers, but still, having the lessons meant that cuts had to be made elsewhere. Josephine couldn't afford to pay for dancing lessons, tap shoes and school shoes. But dancing was Sal's love, so Josephine made a decision – Sal could wear his dancing shoes to school. Of course, this was more fodder for the bullies, and Sal ended up, at the age of ten, with a broken nose.

He didn't care, though, and threw himself into his lessons, putting in six hours a week at the school, and then practising at home.

His first performance came while at the Marie Moser Dance Academy, which had its own Saturday afternoon TV program. Both Sal and Sarina appeared in the show, and shortly afterwards were picked to appear on *The Ted Steele Show,* live from New York.

Even with all of his energies directed towards performing, Sal still managed to get into trouble.

"We were just kids," Sal recalled, "and we were always getting into trouble. It wasn't anything really terrible – mostly things like breaking windows, stealing small things just for the hell of it. I was a hood. The school would call home, or the cops would, and my family couldn't stop me. Finally I got brought into court."

It was this crime that was the making of Sal, however. His gang had sent Sal into the school through a basement window – being the smallest he could fit in through small spaces – and instructed him to steal sports equipment, which he handed to them through the window. With nowhere to hide them, they decided the ideal spot was an empty coffin in Mr Mineo's workshop.

They were caught.

The judge advised Josephine to find a way to channel Sal's energy before he ended up in a correctional facility, and it was decided that Sal would attend an acting school in Manhattan – somewhere that could keep the spirited youngster occupied all day.

One day, in December 1950, Sal was spotted by a casting agent, who gave him his card and told him to be at an audition the following day.

The part he was auditioning for was that of Salvatore, in *The Rose Tattoo*, by Tennessee Williams. He got the part and was given a contract for $75 per week (around $760 today[4]). Sal, the self-proclaimed hood from the Bronx, was earning more than his father.

It wasn't quite the big part he was hoping for, however. Sal's first Broadway appearance saw him chasing a goat across the stage every night, shouting *"The goat is in the yard"*!

Once rehearsals were complete, the play opened in Chicago on December 29th, 1950 and for the first time in his life, Sal was separated from his family.

When the play opened in New York on February 3rd, 1951, Sal was once again able to spend time with his family. Life was better – as soon as he was cast in the play his hellish days of school ended, and his mother hired a private tutor.

The Rose Tattoo won four Tony awards in March 1951, but Sal was restless. His experiences on stage had given him a thirst for the big time – he wanted to be a star. He spent endless days touting for parts, visiting casting agents. He had seen the adoration the actors received, and he wanted it for himself.[5]

Hitting the Big Time

The Rose Tattoo ran for a year, after which Sal had several small parts on the stage – in *Dinosaur Wharf* he played a shoe shiner, but the play closed after only four performances. It was during his stint in *The Little Screwball* at the Westbury Country Playhouse in Connecticut that a talent scout approached him and asked him to audition as an understudy in *The King and I,* for the part of the Crown Prince of Siam, Chulalongkorn.

The play had already been running for more than a year and starred Yul Brynner as the King of Siam. Sal was told he might also have to fill in for any of the actors who played the King's children, none of whom had speaking parts. One night, one of the child actors was sick, so Sal got his first taste of performing at St James' Theater. However, the child whose part Sal was playing was smaller than he was, and as he took a bow during the performance, his belt came undone and his pants fell down.

Unperturbed by the ensuing laughter, Sal's break came in August 1952, when the actor who played Chulalongkorn went on vacation. This was the part Sal had been waiting for – the role required both speaking and singing. It wasn't the performing which worried Sal, though, it was his co-star, Yul Brynner. Because of the part he played as the King of Siam, Brynner came across to the young actor as stern and scary, and this made Sal nervous. So much so that when Sal, who had never had to apply make up for that particular part, was told to ask Brynner for help, he stood at the star's dressing room door, shaking.

His fears were unfounded, though – Brynner proved to be a kind man, who showed Sal the ropes and put him at ease.

"Every night, we would meet in the wings before we went on. He would talk to a 13-year-old boy as an equal. We discussed acting and one day he presented me with several books on the subject," Sal recalled. "At one point during the play's run, I was beginning to have trouble with my part. I was getting mechanical and I wasn't getting what I thought were enough good laughs. One night, I told the King about it. He suggested that we get together and rehearse it again. Immediately, I began getting laughs."

It was the start of an enduring professional friendship between the two actors.

The play closed in 1954, and out of 1,246 performances, Sal had played Chulalongkorn almost 900 times.

The time Sal spent on Broadway was an eye-opener for the young lad. He was frequently targeted by gangsters and young thugs who saw him as a threat, encroaching on their territory. Sal would often have to run the gauntlet of subways in order to lose his pursuers, and more than once he would arrive at the theatre with battle scars and his clothes in disarray.

Sal was an attractive boy in a pretty sort of way, and this brought him unwanted attention from men who were interested in him sexually. He never told his family about these approaches, however, as he thought it might spell the end of his career in acting. Instead, he took care of it himself. John Garfield, Sal's favorite actor at the time, had starred in a movie called *Castle on the Hudson* in which he protected himself by carrying a gun. Young Sal bought himself a toy pistol, which was realistic enough to scare off would-be attackers. It seemed to do the trick.[6]

Away From the Stage

Following *The King and I,* Sal pursued roles on TV. He had several small parts before landing a role in the movie *Six Bridges to Cross*, in which he played the younger version of Tony Curtis' character. It was while he was in Hollywood, working on the dialogue for the movie, that he got himself a part in *The Private War of Major Benson*, about a football coach at a tough boys' military academy.

Rebel Without a Cause

While Sal was working on *Benson*, the opportunity came up to audition in *Rebel Without a Cause*, a movie about angst-ridden teenagers starring James Dean. Sal was eager to land the part of Plato, a sensitive boy who finds himself besotted with James Dean's character, Jim Stark.

Picked for his distinctive looks, at the first audition there was no spark between Mineo and Dean. The director, Nick Ray, suggested the two of them talked and got to know one another.

"I thought I dressed pretty sharp for those days in pegged pants, skinny tie, jacket – until Jimmy Dean walked in with his tee shirt and blue jeans."

After finding common ground, the two hit it off, and when they re-did the scene it flowed. Nick Ray had initial misgivings about casting Sal in the role of Plato, but saw 'something' in him and decided to give him the part.

The film was controversial – the love triangle between Jim Stark, Plato, and Natalie Woods' character Judy, caused more than a few raised eyebrows as the issue of homosexuality was still regarded as 'deviant' – so much so that a kiss between the two male characters was cut by Hollywood Censors. Sal struggled with portraying a man who had homosexual tendencies until James Dean made a suggestion.

"You know how I am with Natalie. Well, why don't you pretend I'm her and you're me? Pretend you want to touch my hair, but you're shy. I'm not shy like you. I love you. I'll touch your hair."

This evidently worked, as the director later remarked that Sal *'broke the sound barrier'* in one particular scene.

Sal clearly had feelings for Dean off-screen, but at the time he was unsure of what they were. Homosexuality wasn't something which was often admitted, especially for a screen idol, although James Dean never made any secret of the fact that he was bisexual.

"If I'd understood back then that a guy could be in love with another one, it would have happened. But I didn't come to that realisation for a few more years and then it was too late for Jimmy and me."

Rebel Without a Cause catapulted Sal into the limelight and established him as a Hollywood heartthrob.

Sal was nominated for an Oscar for 'best supporting actor' for his role as Plato in the film. He was pipped to the post by Jack Lemmon in *Mr Roberts*, but the fact that he had been nominated was an enormous honor and paved the way for more roles.

In *Giant,* Sal played the role of a Mexican boy who was killed during World War II – Angel Obregon II. James Dean also starred in the film although the two actors had no scenes together. *Giant* was, tragically, James Dean's final film performance before his death.

In 1956 Sal played 'Romolo' alongside Paul Newman, in *Somebody Up There Likes Me,* a movie about Rocky Graziano, the boxer.

The same year, Sal was given the part of Angelo "Baby" Gioia in *Crime in the Streets,* a movie about New York Street Gangs. It was this role which saw him earn the nickname 'The Switchblade Kid', and suddenly every boy wanted to be like him, super smooth and cool.

Music

For a while, Sal capitalized on his heartthrob status by launching a career as a recording artist. He was signed to Epic Records and released his first single, *Start Movin'* in 1956. His large fan base ensured the single got to number nine in the charts. His musical career lasted until 1959 – despite his experience in musical theatre Sal was never going to be a singing sensation and in 1959 he returned to acting, playing the part of jazz musician Gene Krupa in *The Gene Krupa Story*.

Back to Acting

After *The Gene Krupa Story*, Sal landed another major role, this one earning him his second Oscar nomination for Best Supporting Actor. In *Exodus*, Sal was cast as Dov Landau, a teenage boy whose entire family had been killed in the Holocaust. His fellow nominees for the Oscar were Chill Wills, Peter Ustinov, Jack Kruschen, and Peter Falk. When Sal lost out to Peter Ustinov for his role in Spartacus, he was devastated. He had become accustomed to being the darling of Hollywood, and he took what he saw as rejection, hard.

It marked the beginning of his demise.

Things Go Downhill

Such was Sal's bitterness towards Ustinov for beating him to the Oscar win that his name was not allowed to be mentioned – any utterance would bring forth a flurry of cursing from the slighted actor.

Things started to fall apart for Sal. He went from living a movie icon lifestyle to that of a bit-part actor, accepting smaller, insignificant roles in order to earn money.

The one silver lining in this period was the film *Who Killed Teddybear?* starring Juliet Prowse, Frank Sinatra's ex-love interest. The film-noir, which was released in 1965, saw Mineo portray a sleazy stalker/voyeur who preyed on Prowse's character. Sal had managed to shake off his typecasting once when he seemed to attract the role of a troubled teenager, but *Teddybear* saw him typecast again, this time as a psychotic felon.

As he fell from the limelight, Sal Mineo was free to discover his sexuality. He embarked on a series of short-term relationships with multiple men, at one point indulging in an affair with Rock Hudson. Rumors surrounding his preferences were thrown around – according to some he had a preference for sadomasochistic sex, and to others, he had a strong attraction to English men.

In 1969, Sal bought the play *Fortune and Men's Eyes* with proceeds from gambling and cast himself as Rocky, a dominant bullying prison inmate who brutally rapes another young prisoner, played by Don Johnson, who was then only 18.

Sal took the decision to prominently and graphically portray the rape in the play – a decision which was lambasted by critics when it opened in Los Angeles' Coronet Theater on January 9th, 1969. However, with a large gay following, Sal's play proved successful enough to open in New York, where Sal directed the play himself. The New York press was more savage, however, and the play closed within a year.

Over the next six years, things went from bad to worse for Mineo. He was barely scraping enough money together from small roles to pay the bills – certainly a far cry from his days as a Hollywood darling. Between 1969 and 1975 he worked in three films, but not even these brought him the praise he was used to.

When the opportunity came up for Sal to audition for a part in Frances Ford Coppola's *The Godfather,* he was sure this was his big break – with his looks and experience the part was surely made for him. However, Coppola thought differently, and rejected him, citing the fact that everyone knew Mineo, as his reason for not casting him.

However, the real reason came to light later on when Coppola admitted that he hadn't given the part to Sal because of his sexuality – a decision he made when a major star in the film told him they objected to *"acting opposite a faggot".*

It soon became clear that Mineo's sexuality was to blame for his lack of good roles – Hollywood was rife with homophobia.

A Brief Reprieve

1976 brought what Sal saw as a new beginning. He had been given the role of Vito, a bisexual burglar in the comedy *P.S. Your Cat is Dead* and once again Mineo's light was shining. Theater critics raved about the show, and Sal's face once again featured in magazines. Life was looking up for Sal, both financially and personally, but his good fortune was not going to last.

Sal's Murder

At 9.30pm on Thursday, February 12th, 1976, Sal Mineo had just returned from rehearsals for *PS Your Cat is Dead*. Several neighbors heard shouts for help and rushed outside to see what was happening. In the carport behind the apartment complex, they found Sal Mineo, curled up in a ball on the ground, and bleeding heavily. Despite being given mouth to mouth by his neighbor, Roy Evans, Sal Mineo died before the paramedics could reach him.

He was 37.

The autopsy on Sal revealed he died from a single stab wound to the heart. At first, detectives pursued the murder as being drug related – the autopsy had also revealed marks on the actor's body which suggested drug use.

When this angle produced no leads, the police then turned their attention to Mineo's sexuality, looking into the possibility that it was a homophobic murder. Many of the industry's gay and bisexual men were interviewed and investigated – the police thinking was that it had been some kind of crime of passion by a jealous or ex-lover. Again that investigation proved fruitless, and the case went cold, much to the fury of the gay community who accused the Los Angeles police of homophobia, a charge vigorously denied by the police department.

The case had been cold for two years when a woman came forward and told police that her husband had killed Mineo.[7] She claimed that he had come home the night of the murder drenched in blood. Lionel Williams was in prison at the time his wife came forward, for bad check charges, and had also been heard bragging to inmates about murdering the actor.

Lionel Williams later retracted his story, but the damage was done and he was convicted of Sal's murder. His motive was robbery.

Speculation was rife surrounding the arrest, however. Witnesses on the night of Sal's death described a man running from the scene – a white man with long brown hair. Lionel Williams was black. However, a photo was unearthed of Williams in which he had straightened his hair and dyed it brown, and this was enough to satisfy the jury that Williams was, indeed, the perpetrator.[8]

Doubt has always surrounded Williams' conviction – did he really stab the actor or was he covering for the real killer? According to Lionel Williams' sister, Sal was murdered over a drug deal. She claimed that he owed thousands of dollars and that her brother was taking the blame for a friend, who she would only refer to as 'Rock' – a military man who had been stationed overseas before the murder, and who returned there shortly afterwards.

In March 1979, rightfully or not, 21-year-old Lionel Williams was sentenced to 51 years to life for second-degree murder, and another ten counts of robbery.[9]

Whether Williams was guilty of the murder or was indeed covering for a friend as his sister claimed, is still debated - 41 years later we are no closer to knowing why, or by whom, Sal Mineo was murdered. Was it homophobia, drugs related, or simply an opportunistic mugging gone wrong?

We will probably never know.

THE MURDER OF ADRIENNE SHELLY

JOSEPH REMAR

Adrienne Shelly was born Adrienne Levine, on June 24th 1966. She was born in Queens, and remained a native of there throughout her childhood. Her parents were Sheldon M. Levine and Elaine Langbaum, and she was raised with her two brothers Jeff and Mark. Her childhood was apparently happy and stable.

Her entrance into the world of the performing arts came at the age of just 10. Her career began at the Stagedoor Manor Performing Arts Training Center, where she learned her craft, before making her professional debut in a rendition of the musical Annie while she was still a high school student. Adrienne took her professional surname (Shelly) from her father's given name, Sheldon. Her father had died when Shelly was aged 12.

After graduation, she left New York for Boston University, where she majored in film production. She didn't enjoy her time there, however, and she dropped out after her junior year and moved back to Manhattan to start her career. Her first forays were into indie movies, and she became reasonably well-known for her femme-fatale characters, although by all accounts, she was more of a "clown" in real life.

Shelly was not just successful in her own right, as her husband was successful too. She married Andy Ostroy, who is still chairman and CEO of Belardi/Ostroy, a marketing firm. The pair met shortly after September 11th, which was a strange time to live in New York. They had been set up on a date by matchmaking friends. "I didn't really know what to make of her at first," Ostroy later recalled. "She was like no one I'd ever met. But I knew right away that she was special. There are very few people in this world who are really unique, and she touched you in a way that meant you could never forget her. It's hard to explain. She had a big smile and a genius IQ."

The couple had a daughter together in 2003, who was named Sophie, and had only turned two by the time that Shelly died. Shelly was killed in a senseless robbery at the apartment she used as her office, late in 2006.

Successful career

Shelly's big break came in 1989, when she was 23 years of age. She was cast in her first leading role in Hal Hartley's independent film, The Unbelievable Truth. Just a year later, she teamed up with Hartley again, this time for the lead role in Trust. Both films were financial successes, and Trust was even nominated for the Grand Jury Prize at the Sundance Film Festival, where Hartley was a joint winner of a scriptwriting award. Meanwhile, Shelly broke through on TV as well as at the box office. She landed roles in several hit TV shows like Law & Order, Oz and Homicide: Life on the Street.

Not content with how well she was doing on screen, Shelly took to the stage, taking on roles in at least two dozen off-Broadway plays. She set up a theater company called Missing Children in 1996. She performed most often at the Manhattan Guesthouse Theater, and played there throughout her long career.

But rather than push on with her well-received start in the film industry, Shelly decided to move instead into roles behind the camera. One of her first successes was I'll Take You There, a 1999 comedy starring Ally Sheedy. For her direction of the movie, Shelly received a U.S. Comedy Arts Festival Film Discovery Jury Award in 2000. She also won Best Director for the same movie at the Tróia International Film Festival.

Her final contribution to film was the movie Waitress. "The central theme of the film is what Adrienne felt in her own life," Shelly's husband told People Magazine. "This story is about a woman who is afraid. It's about a woman who has real challenges and fears in life.

Adrienne was worried that having a child, even though she was still having the child relatively late in life, would jeopardise her career. "There's a moment where Keri Russell finds out that she's pregnant and she's not happy. The doctor even says, 'Uncongratulations.' That was pretty much what Adrienne had feared – that would she lose her identity as a person and her ability to work."

But in a familiar story to parents who at one time had trepidations about having children for the first time, Shelly's outlook completely changed after her daughter's birth. "Once she saw Sophie, it was incredible. The love she had for that child was just monumental. Her fears vanished. She just adored that little girl so much."

And Shelly's fears about being unable to juggle children and career were completely unfounded. "When she started editing the film, she would be in her old apartment where she went to write," he says. "Sophie would be crawling around the floor while she was editing and working on the script. She was joyful about being able to achieve her dreams and still be a mother who was still madly in love with her child. She finally had it all."

The movie was released in 2007, which starred Nathan Fillion and Keri Russell (and Shelly's daughter Sophie, who appeared in a cameo role towards the end of the film). It premiered that year at the Sundance Film Festival. She wrote and directed the movie, and coordinated both set and costume design as well. But unfortunately, she didn't live to see the success of her final creation.

Death ruled suicide

In what was a shock to her family and to the film-going public, Shelly was found dead on the evening of November 1st, 2006. She was discovered in the bathroom of the apartment she used as an office in Manhattan's West Village, hanging from a shower rail with a bedsheet around her neck.

Unfortunately, she was found by her husband, Andy Ostroy. He had suspected that something was amiss; after he had dropped her off early that morning, she hadn't contacted him for the entire day. Ostroy dropped by that evening to see if anything was the matter, and brought the doorman with him in case of intruders.

There were no signs of forced entry, and the door was unlocked, so they went inside. Instead of finding intruders (or indeed anything that might suggest foul play) they found Shelly alone in her apartment, already dead.

Investigations began immediately. The NYPD immediately found that some money had been stolen, or at least home missing, from Shelly's wallet. But they didn't find any other clues that might have suggested anything other than suicide. An autopsy, unsurprisingly, found that the cause of death had been strangulation.

Footprints found

This version of events wasn't enough for Ostroy. He knew for a fact that Shelly had been happy in both her work and her personal life, and that she was the last person who would leave a two year old without a mother. "There's no way on this planet that she would have left that child," he said. "Nobody is ever going to tell me that woman walked away from Sophie." Something didn't add up, and Ostroy pushed the NYPD to resume their analysis of the crime scene.

Taking him at his word, the NYPD did a second sweep of the bathroom for any extra clues. Their efforts revealed something they hadn't seen before: a muddy shoe print, outlined in gypsum powder, on the toilet seat. The pattern didn't match any of Shelly's shoes, nor of Ostroy's; this, therefore, was their first lead. Expanding their search, the NYPD investigators noticed that the print matched another set found elsewhere in the building, where construction work had been taking place on the day of Shelly's death.

They had examined the shoes of every single person who was known to have entered the apartment that day, including even emergency workers and police officers, but had found no matches. They expanded their search to include the rest of the building, and found that the construction work had been taking place; they then noticed that a set of footprints outlined on one of the work sites was a perfect match for the one in Shelly's bathroom.

Worker charged

It took the NYPD five days until they thought they had their man. On November 6th, 2006, Diego Pillco was arrested and charged with the murder of Adrienne Shelly. Pillco was an illegal immigrant, originally from Ecuador, who had been working on the construction site that day. Pillco lived on Prospect Avenue in Greenwood Heights, Brooklyn, at the time that he was arrested. He had only arrived in the city, having come straight from Ecuador, that July. Investigators had tracked him down, and identified him as the wanted man based on the footprints they had found.

He was taken that day from his apartment block, to a waiting police car. The press had already picked up that this may have been the man suspected of Shelly's murder- so Pillco left the building escorted by police officers, wearing a Yankees cap low over his face to avoid photographers.

Investigators reported that he had confessed to the murder. "He admits to hitting her, believes he had killed her and wanted to fake her suicide," one of the investigators told the press the day after Pillco's arrest. He asked not to be named since investigations were, at that point, still continuing. "It appeared to be a suicide — he staged it as a suicide," the investigator said. But his team had "never just accepted it for what it was staged to be."

Speaking after Pillco had been charged, Shelly's agent Rachel Sheedy said: "We have felt adamantly that what happened was not the result of suicide. It is a great relief knowing that the police have taken us seriously." Neighbors of Pillco's also spoke to the press, shortly after he was first charged. They expressed their shock at the difference between the criminal that they read about in the newspapers, and the neighbor they had lived next to all that time.

"He sent money home to his mother and father," said Frank Lingo, who lived nearby. "He minded his business. He never bothered me or anyone else near here. He seemed like a good kid. I've never seen him hang out." Chris Pannhorse, another of Pillco's neighbors, told the press that "He was always respectful to me and my wife. He's a good kid. Because that is what he is to me, just a kid."

What had happened that day?

According to Pillco's initial version of events, Shelly had asked him to 'keep the noise down' since she had been working in her office that day. Taking offence to her, Pillco threw a hammer at her out of anger. Pillco had been working on an apartment on the third floor, directly below the apartment that Shelly used as her office.

He confessed that because of his poor grasp of English, he had been unable to fully understand what she was saying; but he had picked up on the fact that she had threatened to call the police. After she had run back to her apartment, Pillco followed her. He said that he had been afraid she would make a complaint to his superior, or to call 911, which would result in his sacking and the revelation of his status as an illegal immigrant.

Out of fear, therefore, Pillco said that he had killed Shelly that day. In the ensuing struggle once they reached her office, Shelly hit him, but Pillco hit back harder, and Shelly fell awkwardly and died. He was unsure as to whether the blow had killed her, but nevertheless, he confessed to staging the scene to make it appear like a simple suicide.

Friends and family of Shelly were grateful to Ostroy, as they felt that none of the real story would have come out had it not been for his efforts in convincing investigators to look harder. "He was her hero," a friend of Shelly, Sasha Eden, told the press, "even in her death. Andy did everything in his power, and made the whole murder come out."

Conflicting stories

However, by the time of his trial, Pillco's story had changed entirely. In truth, Pillco's first story did seem to be inconsistent in places: for instance, while he claimed that Shelly had come screaming into the building site that he was working on, Shelly's shoes had been completely clean when they were assessed by investigators.

He initially plead not guilty, but eventually gave damning testimony against himself during proceedings after agreeing to a plea bargain. He later said that he had simply seen her while he was on his break, and taken the elevator to her apartment with the intent of either assaulting her or stealing her purse: he was never completely clear.

Finding that she wasn't there, Pillco decided to take advantage of the situation. He rifled through Shelly's purse, stealing some money; but he was discovered in the act. Shelly confronted him, and perhaps scratched him; similarly to events in his first confession, she then picked up the phone to try to call 911. Pillco grabbed the phone to stop her.

But Shelly wasn't afraid to call for help, and Pillco hit her hard, knocking her to the ground.

"So out of desperation, I got scared and I covered her mouth," Pillco told the packed courtroom during his trial. It was this that had rendered Shelly unconscious. "When I noticed she fell to the floor, I was very scared. When she fell to the floor, I saw a sheet, and I decided to choke her — and that's what happened." The judge cut across him to ask: "And then you tied the sheet around her neck and you strung her up?"

"Si," Pillco replied. "Yes, and I made it look like it was suicide."

After strangling her until she was unconscious, he set up the fake suicide scene. It was the weight of her body pulling the bed sheet tight around her neck that eventually killed her. This was confirmed at trial by the medical examiner, who stated that Shelly had been alive at the time she was left hanging in the bathroom; it had therefore been the cover-up that had killed her, not the initial fight.

Because he had not delivered the final killing blow, Pillco was offered a plea of first degree manslaughter. Prosecutors feared that they may have been unsuccessful if they tried to find him guilty of murder, because of the chance that he would switch to his original story again.

It almost seemed too soon after proceedings had begun, just four months earlier, for the trial to be at an end in February. He had been offered a plea by the Manhattan district attorney, who recognised the shakiness of Pillco's story. In return for pleading guilty to a charge of first-degree manslaughter, he would receive a set sentence of 25 years. Considering that he could have potentially been found guilty of murder in a trial by jury, Pillco's lawyers insisted that he grab the offer with both hands.

Pillco, for his part, did show remorse at the end of the hearings. "If there were a death penalty, I would take it," he told the courtroom though an interpreter.. "All I want to say is I know they're not going to forgive me. This is what I deserve." But Shelly's family, who were in the courtroom looking down at Pillco, couldn't have appeared any less forgiving. Elaine was sobbing, wiping her eyes, and hissing "No... No!"-

she could not forgive the man who had murdered her daughter. Neither could any other member of her family, nor could Andy Ostroy- it was simply too soon.

In response to Pillco's please for forgiveness, even the judge retorted: "I don't think you'll get that, sir."

It seemed so senseless, and so strange that a man who could show such remorse could have killed Shelly the way that he had. But according to the evidence, testimony and his own confessions, he had committed the crime. He was given a sentence of 25 years, with no chance of parole, and a practical guarantee that he would be deported back to Ecuador upon his release.

Ostroy speaks out against his wife's killer

During the hearing at which Pillco's sentence was handed down, Andy Ostroy was given a chance to speak his mind- and he took his chance to express the anger, hurt and loss he had felt after his wife's senseless murder. "No sentence will be enough for you. You deserve the same fate you handed Adrienne. I want you to suffer like she suffered."

"You are nothing more than a cold-blooded killer, a murderous beast who in an intent to rob, rape and then silence your innocent victim ... took the life of a beautiful, loving woman who, unlike you, had so much to give to society," he said, glaring down at Pillco, who couldn't meet his gaze.

"You stalked and brutally attacked my wife, silenced her screams with your hand until you rendered her unconscious and then, in a brutal and gruesome act of cowardice, took a bedsheet and strangled her to death," Ostroy said, still staring as if unable to wrench his eyes away from his wife's killer. "You tied her up and hung her the way you strung up pigs back in Ecuador."

Shelly's mother, Elaine Langbaum, was also given a chance to speak. She used her time to talk about how Shelly and her daughter, after such a perfect start in life, had been robbed of their chance to grow older together. "The baby she wanted for so long will never know her mother," she said. "She will never hold her mother's hand, kiss her mother's face or feel her mother's hug."

Ostroy sues the construction company

After taking time to grieve, and recover as much as he could, Ostroy decided that he hadn't finished trying to make sense of Shelly's death. He has described himself as "a born and bred New Yorker- push me and I'll push back harder," and he felt a need to find justice. He decided to sue the construction company that had hired Pillco, and demanded a settlement for a charge of negligence.

However, the Appellate Division of the Manhattan court system decided to uphold the earlier decision ruling against Ostroy's suit. They unanimously judged that the construction company were innocent of the charge, since murder was not a part of Pillco's job description, and therefore his actions could not be judged the liability of the company. The judges agreed that there was no way that the construction company could have identified Pillco's propensity for violence upon hiring him, and that he had been furthering his own interests in killing Shelly, not those of the company.

While in hindsight, a successful suit always seemed unlikely, Ostroy's actions make sense in the context of grief and loss. He had lashed out in an attempt to find somebody else to blame. Pillco was in prison, having been found guilty, and even having shown remorse; but his crime had been so mindless, shocking and unpredictable that it must have been difficult for the family to make sense of his actions.

Waitress

Shelly's final movie, Waitress, was also her final and best success. It premiered at the Sundance Film Festival in 2007, to a rapturous reception. "Seeing Waitress at Sundance was a really emotional experience," said Nancy Utley, a CEO at Fox Searchlight, which was one of the distributers that had bid for rights to the film. "The typical format for the festival is that the director is introduced to say a few words before the film begins. It was painful from the beginning to see that there was no director to introduce the film, since Adrienne had passed away. So the producer and Adrienne's husband Andy talked about how it had been Adrienne's dream to have a film at Sundance. It was very poignant."

According to Utley, the film was exceptionally well-received. "The movie played like gangbusters. The audience was laughing and crying, and sometimes both at the same time. There was a standing ovation at the end." There was also a political/societal point that could be made of the film: Shelly had written, edited and directed Waitress while pregnant and just after having given birth. This was in addition to all the challenges that she, as a woman, had to overcome. "No one questions Woody Allen or Christopher Guest," Sasha Eden said after the movie's success. "But when you're a woman it's much more challenging. Here was this gorgeous writer-director-actor who had to constantly prove that she could do it."

The movie's producer, Michael Roiff, completely agreed. "One of the things she was most excited about was the fact that she had done this as a woman and as a mother. She was an amazing mum, and I remember one day when we had watched a cut of the film, she turned around and said: "Look, you can do it. Society wants to tell you that you have to choose, but you don't have to choose."

During the movie's success, Broadway producers Barry and Fran Weissler saw a screening and decided to turn it into a musical number. The show was a hit. "When I found out it was heading to Broadway, I was thrilled," Ostroy said afterwards "When I look at Adrienne's life, career and legacy, she had this film that did really well, is now on Broadway and she has impacted the lives of so many female filmmakers. I have seen that out of tragedy, something really good can come, otherwise it's all in vain. Her murder didn't stop her from going on, even if in name only."

Ostroy and Sophie have since seen the show, and described it as "a wonderful addition to Adrienne's legacy. It's one of the many things she has to remember about her mother as she is growing up."

Shelly's foundation

Shelly's husband was also determined that some good should come from his wife's early death. "For a few weeks after she died, I had a lot of people who were asking where they could donate money in her honor," he says. "It was too soon. I didn't know. Those first few weeks were harrowing and I wanted to think about it. When my head was able to get clearer, I thought, 'What would Adrienne want? Who would Adrienne want to help?' Other struggling women filmmakers."

"'I think Adrienne would be very proud that in her name other women are being helped in ways that she wished she could have been. Given what happened to her, there's so much positive that can come out of it - that's the reason behind the foundation: to try to take something horrible and make something positive."

He set up a foundation in her name, the aim of which was to provide women in the showbusiness industry with a leg-up that could help their careers. The board are such Hollywood stars as Cheryl Hines, Paul Rudd and Michelle Williams, and so far the foundation has teamed up with production studios and organisations like the American Film Institute, the Sundance Film Festival, Women in Film, the Tribeca Film Institute and Rooftop Films.

They have given out at least 60 production grants since the foundation's inception, one of the most successful being a grant for filmmaker Cynthia Wade in 2007. The grant helped her to release the documentary film Freeheld, which was given an Academy Award. Speaking about his organisation's helping hand for Cynthia Wade, Ostroy claimed: "She said she couldn't have made that film without our support. To help a filmmaker win an Academy Award with help from our foundation made us realize the impact that we could have – and so soon."

He continued, "Starting the foundation was the right thing to do for Adrienne and the right thing to do, period. I think Adrienne would have loved that we are helping filmmakers like her in her honor and in her name."

THE MURDER OF DOMINIQUE DUNNE

ERICA THOMAS

Destined for stardom

In November 1959, film producer Dominick Dunne and actress Ellen (Lenny) Dunne welcomed a new baby to their growing family. Dominique Dunne was the couple's youngest of three children, and their only daughter. Dunne and her older brothers grew up surrounded by the arts – in addition to the influence of their parents, who were active in the California film industry, the children were frequently surrounded by celebrities of the 50s and 60s – close family friends who were often guests at the family home.

Dunne and her siblings grew up in a large house in Beverly Hills, but moved around fairly frequently as Dunne attended schools across the country – in Los Angeles, Connecticut, and Colorado. However, Dunne's childhood wasn't entirely carefree – when she was just eleven years old, Dunne's parents divorced. A few years later, in 1975, her mother was diagnosed with multiple sclerosis.

Still, Dunne pursued her education. After her graduation in 1977, Dunne studied art and Italian in Florence, at the Michelangelo School and at the British Institute. When she returned to California, she worked briefly as a receptionist and translator for Los Angeles' Italian Trade Commission before venturing back to Ft. Collins to study acting at the Colorado State University.

Her studies in Colorado were short-lived, however, and Dunne left after only one year to start auditioning back in California. Just a few weeks later, she was offered her very first film role. Dunne's acting career took off quite quickly – in her first three years, Dunne appeared as a guest on many well-known television shows, including *Family*, *CHiPs*, and *Fame*. And after taking on roles in four made-for-TV movies, Dunne made her cinematic debut as Dana Freeling in the movie "Poltergeist."

"One day, she decided to become an actress and the next week she was on a back lot making a movie, and that from then on she never stopped," said Dunne's father Dominick in a piece he wrote for Vanity Fair in March 1984. "She loved being an actress and was passionate about her career."

"At ease in a sophisticated world."

To her friends and family, Dunne was known as a friendly, kind person. Despite having grown up with wealth and fame, Dunne's father described her as "totally at ease in a sophisticated world without being sophisticated herself." Indeed, Dunne dressed in casual clothes, preferring jeans and t-shirts to the upscale fashions her peers sported – and drove a blue Volkswagen Bug convertible.

Dunne loved cooking, traveling, baseball, and languages – particularly Italian, which she continued to speak quite fluently. She also loved animals, and had a soft spot for unwanted strays. Dunne adopted a cat with a lobotomy, a large dog with stunted legs, a snake, and a rabbit, among many other cats and dogs.

Even before her role in "Poltergeist," Dunne was a firm believer in supernatural phenomena, and friends say she was strictly superstitious.

Instant attraction

Dunne met John Thomas Sweeney in 1981, when she was twenty-two and he was twenty-five. Sweeney worked as a chef at Los Angeles' trendy "Ma Maison" restaurant, and Dunne was immediately drawn to him. After their initial introduction at a party that autumn, the pair quickly fell into a romantic relationship – and moved in together only a few weeks later, into a rental house in West-Hollywood.

However, their passion soon resulted in the first of many quarrels between the couple. Dunne was, by that point, well-known in Hollywood – a popular girl with many friends. Sweeney, on the other hand, had grown up poor in Pennsylvania, the product of a troubled family life. Despite Dunne's attempts to include him in her world, Sweeney felt like an outsider and was ashamed of his uncultured family history.

While Dunne had grown up with a loving family that respected and addressed emotional issues, Sweeney was raised in a coal town with an alcoholic father who, his mother claimed, often dealt with his frustrations by beating her – often in front of their children. By the time he was fourteen years old, his parents had divorced, and his father had developed epilepsy.

"Bitterly ashamed of his family and filled with a sense of worthlessness because he was a member of it, (Sweeney) longed to escape into a larger and more exciting life," read an article published in *People* magazine in 1983.

Sweeney's desire for a better life led him to pursue a culinary arts diploma from a local community college. At the age of twenty, he crossed the country to California, where he landed a job working at a restaurant called "Picolo's." Only one year later, he started as a chef's apprentice at "Ma Maison."

He was a talented, ambitious chef – and was willing to put in the work to achieve his career goals. After two years of double shifts, Sweeney was given a leave of absence to spend a year working on the French Riviera before returning to "Ma Maison" – where he worked as chef Wolfgang Puck's chief assistant.

His position at the glamorous restaurant gave him an opportunity to get a first-hand look at the elegant world he so desperately wanted to be a part of. And, after meeting Dunne, he finally felt like he would be able to access it. However, along with his excitement at being with a talented Hollywood actress, there was fear and insecurity – and the lasting sense of worthlessness he felt as a result of his troubled family life.

His jealousy started to take hold of the relationship. His interactions with Dunne grew more patronizing and dominating, and he began showing up on sets where Dunne was working to intimidate her male colleagues. Eventually, even that wasn't enough – Sweeney started to come to Dunne's rehearsals and even her acting classes.

It seemed Dunne couldn't do anything on her own without having to first discuss it with her boyfriend, which usually resulted in an argument that Dunne would never win. The more Dunne resisted Sweeney's possessiveness and jealousy, the more frightened he would be that she would ultimately reject him. Often, this fear would become anger.

"Alex said he was scary."

Dunne had introduced Sweeney to her family during the summer of 1982, flying the two of them out to New York where most of her family lived. According Dominick's article in Vanity Fair, Dunne's brother Alex was the only one who had "voiced his dislike" of her new boyfriend.

"Although I could see that Sweeney was excessively devoted to her, there was something off-putting about him," Dominick said.

The first night, Alex told his father about an incident that had happened after Dominick had left the restaurant. Dunne had been recognized by a man in the bar, who called out her iconic line from the film "Poltergeist." According to Alex, "there was no flirtation," just an excited, if slightly tipsy, fan.

"When Sweeney returned to the table and saw the man talking to (Dunne), he became enraged. He picked up the man and shook him," stated Dominick. "Alex said that Sweeney's reaction was out of all proportion to the incident going on. Alex said he was scary."

The next day, Dominick was to meet Dunne and Sweeney for lunch. Although he said he arrived at the restaurant late, the couple still wasn't there – and Dominick was already on his second bottle of Perrier by the time his daughter showed up with her boyfriend.

"I was immediately aware that she had been crying, and that there was tension between them," Dominick said. "The lunch was not a success. I found Sweeney ill at ease, nervous, difficult to talk to. It occurred to me that (Dunne) might have difficulty extricating herself from such a person, but I did not pursue the thought."

Getting physical

As the couple began fighting more and more, Sweeney's reactions frequently turned violent. On August 27, 1982, Sweeney reportedly tore out handfuls of Dunne's hair after grabbing it and using it to knock her head repeatedly against the floor. Dunne managed to get away from Sweeney and fled to her mother Lenny's house, with Sweeney following close behind. While Dunne's mother refused him entry and even threatened to call the police, it was only a few days before Dunne forgave her boyfriend and returned to their home.

Despite Dunne's forgiveness, Sweeney attacked her again not even a month later. On September 26, during another argument, Sweeney grabbed Dunne by the neck and pushed her to the floor before he started to choke her. Luckily, a friend heard the loud gagging noises coming from the next room – "it was the worst sound I had ever heard" – and came in to break up the fight.

"He tried to kill me!" Dunne cried out. Sweeney denied her accusation, insisting that Dunne come back to bed. Instead, she went into the bathroom, where she escaped out a window to spend the night with a friend.

The next day, Dunne showed up at the set of *Hill Street Blues*, where she was to guest star as an abuse victim for an episode of the show. According to accounts from cast and crew on the set, the bruises on Dunne's face and neck were "realistic" enough that she hardly needed any make-up for her role.

Dunne spent the following days in hiding, trying to avoid the abusive, angry boyfriend who was searching for her. Eventually, she contacted him to end the relationship – and to demand he leave the home they rented together so she could live there alone. Still, knowing how unpredictably angry and violent Sweeney could be, Dunne changed the locks of the house before moving back in without him.

The final battle

That autumn, Dunne had taken on a new role – playing Robin Maxwell for the three-episode science fiction miniseries *V.* She'd completed filming the scenes for the first episode and was nearly finished with the second episode on October 30, when she invited her co-star David Packer to rehearse scenes together at her home.

The pair were hard at work when Sweeney called Dunne at around 8:30 p.m. – and then showed up at the house only ten minutes later. Dunne answered the door with the chain fastened, but Sweeney demanded she come out and speak with him. Packer asked if he should leave, sensing Dunne's discomfort with the situation, but she said she wanted him to stay while she stepped outside to deal with her ex-boyfriend.

Out on the driveway, an argument broke out. Sweeney was pleading with Dunne to forgive him and take him back, but Dunne refused. She'd reached her limit and was no longer willing to tolerate Sweeney's anger and violence. Like he'd done before, Sweeney suddenly reached out and grabbed her firmly by the neck, dragging her up along the driveway into the next-door neighbour's back yard.

Dunne was no match for Sweeney – the petite actress was a mere 5'1" and 112 pounds. Sweeney, 6'1" and close to 200 pounds, held her down and began to strangle her. She was unable to fight him off, and eventually fell unconscious.

Meanwhile, Packer watched the confrontation with growing fear – he could see Sweeney's obvious rage and jealousy. When he heard screams followed by a thud, he called the police, only to be informed that the location was outside of the department's jurisdiction. After hanging up with the officer, Packer called a friend and left a message on his answering machine explaining that if he was found dead, John Sweeney should be held responsible.

Eventually, Packer went outside to check on Dunne, and found her lying on the driveway with Sweeney crouched next to her. Sweeney asked Dunne to call the police, and this time, they said they would send an officer. When the police arrived and found Dunne still unconscious, they called an ambulance, which arrived only five minutes later.

Brain-dead

On the way to the nearby Cedars Sinai Hospital, Dunne's heart came to a full stop, but doctors were able to restart it once the ambulance arrived. However, examinations showed that Dunne had sustained extensive damage from the anoxaemia during her strangulation – and that although her heart had been restarted, there was no way for doctors to reverse the death of her brain.

"There were tubes in her everywhere, and the life-support system caused her to breathe in and out with a grotesque jerking movement that seemed a parody of life," Dominick recalled. "Her eyes were open, massively enlarged, staring lifelessly up at the ceiling. Her beautiful hair had been shaved off. A large bolt had been screwed into her skull to relieve the pressure on her brain. Her neck was purpled and swollen; vividly visible on it were the marks of the massive hands of the man who had strangled her.

It was nearly impossible to look at her, but also impossible to look away."

The hospital's staff did everything they could for Dunne, and after five days, her parents made the decision to remove her from the life-support systems that were keeping her alive. Dunne died instantly, and her heart and kidneys were donated to the hospital to be used for transplants.

Dunne's tragic death was a shock to the entire Hollywood community, particularly for Dunne's extensive network of family and friends. Hundreds of people attended Dunne's funeral, held on November 6 at the catholic Church of the Good Shepherd in Beverly Hills – the same church where Dunne had been baptized 22 years earlier. Her body was laid to rest near Los Angeles, at the Westwood Memorial Park.

"An act of passion and despair."

"If (Dunne) had been killed in an automobile accident, horrible as that would have been, at least it would have been over and mourning could have begun," Dominick said. "A murder is an ongoing event until the day of the sentencing, and mourning has to be postponed."

Sweeney was charged with Dunne's murder, and the case finally went to trial at the court in Santa Monica in early August, 1983. A *People* magazine article from October 1983 described Sweeney as a "young man in a black suit" seated at a long table, his face "white as an egg" and his large, pale hands "folded meekly" over a Bible.

"It is the fashion among the criminal fraternity to find God, and Sweeney, the killer, was no exception," Dominick remembered. "The Bible was a prop; Sweeney never read it, he just rested his folded hands on it. He also wept regularly. One day, the court had to be recessed because he claimed the other prisoners had been harassing before he entered, and he needed time to cry in private.

"I could not believe that the jurors would buy such a performance."

But Sweeney painted a very different picture in the courtroom than the true colors he'd shown to Dunne's family and friends. According to Sweeney's testimony, Dunne "provoked" the violent struggle that resulted in her death, because she had previously agreed to reconcile and had then refused to take Sweeney back. Sweeney said he "just exploded and lunged toward her" after she told him she'd been lying when she said she would live with him again.

He added that he "had no memory" of the event, only that he found himself next to Dunne's unconscious body, with his hands pressed around her neck. According to Sweeney, he tried to resuscitate her, and when that didn't work, he ran into the house and swallowed two bottles of pills – attempting suicide due to his panic and regret at what he had done.

Sweeney's lawyer Michael Adelson added that Dunne was a "snob," who was constantly telling Sweeney how he was beneath her. Sweeney's account of their relationship presented Dunne as two-faced and heartless, and he said she even told him that she had been leading him on.

Dominick even recalled receiving a phone call from the prosecutor for the case, district attorney Steven Barshop, in July, shortly before the trial was set to begin. Barshop explained that Adelson had requested that Lenny not be allowed in the courtroom – Adelson felt the presence of the victim's mother, confined to a wheelchair, would create "undue sympathy for her that would be prejudicial to Sweeney."

The "accident" was a "tragedy," Adelson argued, "not a real crime – an action of passion and despair."

However, no evidence could be found to back up Sweeney's story, and investigators were reluctant to believe him. There was nothing to support Sweeney's claim that he'd attempted to commit suicide, and even during his initial interrogation, Sweeney seemed to show little remorse for his part in Dunne's death.

In fact, the police officers who arrested him testified that Sweeney had seemed "quite calm and collected," and more concerned about what would happen to him than what had happened to Dunne – only about an hour and a half after he'd been arrested.

"I fucked up, I can't believe I did something that will put me behind bars forever," Sweeney reportedly told police when he was brought down to the station. "Man, I blew it. I killed her. I didn't think I choked her that hard. I just kept on choking her. I just lost my temper and blew it again."

When one of the officers made a comment about how well Dunne had been doing with her acting career, Sweeney retorted, "well, I was doing quite well in *my* career. I'm quite proud of what I've done."

Upon further investigation, it was revealed that Sweeney had obviously strangled Dunne for about five minutes – at least four minutes, according to the medical examiner. According to police, this makes Sweeney's story fairly improbable. Not only would Sweeney have had enough time to realize what he was doing while he was choking his ex-girlfriend, he would have had the opportunity to regain control and let Dunne live.

During the trial, Dominick remembers Barshop holding up a hand to the jury, silencing the room for a four-minute period – "how long it took for Dominique Dunne to die," Barshop said, in his opening statement.

"It was horrifying," Dominick said. "I had never allowed myself to think how long she had struggled in his hands, thrashing for life. A gunshot or a knife stab is over in an instant; strangulation is an eternity."

Barshop also brought forward testimony from one of Sweeney's previous girlfriends – a secretary named Lillian Pierce, who'd also lived with Sweeney. During their relationship, which lasted from 1977 to

1980, he'd abused her on at least ten different occasions – resulting in two separate hospital visits, one for a perforated eardrum and collapsed lung, and a second time with a broken nose.

"Later, we heard that (Pierce) had sat in a car outside the church at (Dunne's) funeral and cried," Dominick said, "feeling too guilty to go inside."

The testimony proved that unlike what Sweeney's lawyer had argued, this was not a unique crime of passion, but rather a pattern of abusive behaviour toward women. Still, Sweeney's lawyer was able to convince the judge that the testimony was prejudicial, and had it excluded from the trial.

"Her account of her relationship with John Sweeney was so shocking that it should have put to rest forever the defense stand that the strangulation death of Dominique Dunne at the hands of John Sweeney was an isolated incident," wrote Dominick. "He was, it became perfectly apparent, a classic abuser of women – and his weapon was his hands."

As he questioned Pierce, without the jury present, Adelson inquired about a specific discussion the witness had had with himself and another lawyer on November 3, 1982 – the day before Dunne was officially removed from life-support and pronounced legally dead.

"Even while (Dunne) lay dying, efforts were being made to free her killer by men who knew very well that this was not his first display of violence," Dominick said. "I felt hatred for Michael Adelson. His object was to win; nothing else mattered."

Testimonies from Dunne's friends and co-workers were also ruled out after Sweeney's lawyer argued that they were nothing but hearsay. These statements explained that Dunne was not remotely interested in a reconciliation with Sweeney – in fact, she'd spent the final five weeks of her life in "permanent fear" of her abusive ex-boyfriend.

Even without this important evidence, the prosecution still sought a second-degree murder conviction, with a minimum sentence of fifteen years.

The jury did get to hear a letter found by Dunne's friends, addressed to Sweeney but obviously never sent to him. The letter detailed Dunne's frustrations at the control Sweeney attempted to hold over her, and her desire to end the relationship.

"You do not love me. You are obsessed with me. The person you think you love is not me at all. It is someone you have made up in your head," Dunne said in her letter. "I'm the person who makes you angry, who you fight with sometimes. I think we only fight when images of me fade away and you are faced with the real me.

"The whole thing has made me realize how scared I am of you, and I don't mean just physically. I'm afraid of the next time you are going to have another mood swing. When we are good, we are great. But when we are bad, we are horrendous. The bad outweighs the good."

An unsatisfying result

The trial wrapped up at the end of September, and the jury found Sweeney guilty of voluntary manslaughter – to the shock of Dunne's family and friends. "The law protected him," the jury said, but several members later admitted that had they known about Sweeney's history of violence and abuse, they would have found him guilty of the second-degree murder charge.

"I guess there is never any real satisfaction that the legal system can give, but this – the outcome – was such a blow, such a slap in the face to our family and to (Dunne's) memory," said Dunne's older brother Griffin. "They literally got away with murder... the bitterness of that will never leave."

Even Superior Court Judge Burton S. Katz, who presided over the trial, felt the system failed to provide justice for Dunne's tragic murder. Barshop stated that this failure has allowed a "time bomb" to return to the streets, where he could potentially abuse again, and blames Katz for the many rulings he made that prohibited the jury from hearing important, relevant evidence.

However, Katz argued that he had no choice but to rule the way he had – but admitted that some of the more controversial rulings during the trial "pained" him. Shortly after Sweeney's trial, Katz moved to the Juvenile Court in Sylmar.

"Nothing is more difficult than rendering a decision based upon a law with which you disagree," Katz said. "Unfortunately, following the letter of the law sometimes doesn't permit one to pursue the ultimate goal of justice."

Sweeney ended up with a sentence of only six and a half years in prison, the maximum sentence imposed for convictions of voluntary manslaughter. Instead of the fifteen years the prosecution had hoped for, Sweeney was released from a medium-security state prison after spending three years, seven months, and twenty-seven days in custody.

"Three and a half years for a life is certainly not justice," Katz said. "If I could have given him 25 (years), I would have given him 25. If I could have given him life, I would have given him life... I agree with everyone that based on his past record of violence... he is dangerous to any woman."

Soon after his release from prison, Sweeney found another high-paying job as a head chef at a chic restaurant in Santa Monica called "The Chronicle." The new position didn't last long, though - Sweeney was fired after Dunne's family and friends descended on the restaurant with handbills that were distributed to guests and passers-by.

"The hands that prepared your food strangled Dominique Dunne on October 30, 1982," the handbills read.

Sweeney left Los Angeles for Seattle in 1989, and changed his name to John Maura. According to some sources, he is currently employed there as an executive chef for a chain restaurant.

"This guy gets to be reinstated as the head chef in a restaurant as if nothing ever happened," said Dunne's older brother, actor Griffin

Dunne. "If she had lived, she'd be an actress everyone in the world would know... he's a murderer; he's murdered and I think he will do it again."

Another friend of the family echoed these thoughts, adding that "the verdict almost says it's okay to kill the one you love."

THE MURDER OF LANA CLARKSON

NINA LANE

Hollywood is a place where everything is possible. It is a land of dreams and people flock to this city on the west coast in order to find a better life and create a brighter future for them. Unfortunately, Hollywood has its dark and seedy side as well. Starting with the murder of the Black Dahlia, the tabloids couldn't get enough of intriguing stories coming straight from this part of Los Angeles.

Just like the majority of California girls, Lana Clarkson wanted to become famous. She had that superstar look and when her family moved to Los Angeles, Lana did her best to make a name for herself in the entertainment industry. She had no idea that an accidental encounter with a world famous producer and mad musical genius Phil Spector will be fatal and end her hopes and dreams of international fame. So let's dive a little bit deeper into their lives and everything that preceded this unfortunate event that captured the public's attention in the 2000s.

Early life

Lana Clarkson was born on 5th of April, 1962 in Long Beach, California. She grew up in a large family that included both parents, one brother, and one sister. They were very close because of the small age gap between the siblings. Lana focused on her education and was moderately successful, attending Pacific Union College and she didn't even think about Hollywood fame back in those days. Everything changed for the Clarkson family after the death of their father. They relocated to Los Angeles in hopes of finding better employment opportunities.

Hollywood values youth and beauty so it was clear that Lana will fit right in. Her height and beautiful long blonde hair made her incredibly attractive. Since she was already in Los Angeles, she had a perfect opportunity to try her luck and audition for a couple of movie roles. She was 5"11" which is the perfect height for modeling so Lana made a decision to enter the world of fashion and see how it goes. Lana had the supermodel look and was quickly noticed by modeling agencies. She appeared in numerous spreads but didn't achieve the worldwide fame. However, she made a name for herself in Los Angeles and Lana though it might be the perfect time to launch her movie career.

Breakthrough

The movie industry was blossoming in the 1980s with numerous huge blockbusters getting released every single month. The competition was tough and sometimes all you needed was a bit of luck to get the best role that would launch you to stardom. Since Lana was already a model, she was offered non-speaking roles in the very beginning of her acting career. You could see her in the background of many movies and TV shows of that time. She was stunning and you simply couldn't take your eyes off her.

Her first big acting job was in *Fast Times at Ridgemont High*. It was a small movie at that time but it now has a cult status. Her role wasn't prominent and Lana appeared in just a couple of scenes. But it was enough to get noticed by acclaimed Hollywood producers who are always on a lookout for new stars. She had a couple smaller roles in 1982 but her career was launched once she became Roger Corman's favorite muse.

Roger Corman's movies were aimed at teenagers and often included fantasy characters that relied on their physical appearance. Lana's beauty and height were an ideal combination and Corman decided to give her a supporting role in *Deathstalker*. She played a strong female warrior and it was clear she was perfect for that role. *Barbarian Queen* was her next movie and it was obvious that she found her niche. Corman's movies weren't super successful back in the 1980s, but they did have a large following even then and Lana was a fan favorite. Her body was simply amazing and she looked incredibly good in the costumes. She wasn't shy and often filmed nude scenes.

Lana continued making similar movies all throughout that decade. She did appear in a sequel to *Barbarian Queen*. That movie also included tiny costumes and nudity which were the recurring details in these fantasy flicks.

Lana Clarkson was a humanitarian and would often volunteer for charity organizations. As a matter of fact, Lana was one of the first celebrities who offered her help to those suffering from AIDS and HIV. The disease itself wasn't well researched back then and the public was generally afraid of the virus. Lana didn't care about it and would deliver food to patients in the Los Angeles area.

She made a turn in the 1990s and decided to start accepting horror movie roles. Fantasy and horror would often overlap and her role in *Haunting of Morella* was particularly interesting because she played a lesbian character. Lana continued to model and she would often travel all around the world which did have an impact on her movie career. She didn't get too many roles in the 1990s but continued to make guest appearances on various TV shows.

The movies she made with Corman were still popular and Lana would appear at conventions with rest of the cast. She had a following and they adored her. Lana treated her fans with a lot of respect and she was genuinely happy to sing autographs and speak to them. Unfortunately, her fame started to fade away as Lana got older. After all, the majority of her roles depended on her stunning body and youthful looks. Luckily, Lana accepted the modern technology and she launched her own website for the fans. She would sell merchandise and various autographed items. The pay wasn't enormous but it was enough for her.

Lana planned to reinvent her career in the beginning of 2000. She started taking classes and wanted to land her first comedic role. She opened her own production house called Living Doll Productions and was looking forward to creating and starring in her own movie projects. Unfortunately, she lacked funds and decided to take up some extra work. She became a hostess at the House of Blues. The House of Blues is one of the most popular places on the Sunset Boulevard in the very heart of Los Angeles. Many celebrities party there and it is co-owned by Dan Aykroyd. Phil Spector, who was a famous music producer that revolutionized rock n roll music was a regular guest there.

The infamous producer

Phil Spector was born on 26th of December 1939. After spending his early childhood in Bronx, New York, his family moved to Los Angeles and Phil became interested in making music. He became somewhat famous with this band The Teddy Bears. The duo had a hit song in 1958 but Phil soon came to realize that he had a bad case of stage fright and his performances were influenced greatly by it. Instead of working on getting over that problem, Phil focused on producing and he invented the so-called wall of sound which will make him well-known among musicians.

Over the course of the 1960s, Phil collaborated with numerous stars, bringing a whole new perspective to their music and providing them with fresh and innovative ideas. He was a manager to some of the most well-known bands of the decade such as the Ronettes. Spector worked with the Beatles and was John Lennon's favorite producer. As the years passed by, Spector started to become a recluse, carefully picking out his new projects and musicians to collaborate with. Spector was a short man who would often dress up in unusual clothing and he loved wearing wigs. His recognizable sound wasn't as popular as before during the 1990s but Spector continued to lead a wild life, going out every single night and retreating to his so-called castle in Alhambra which is a suburb of Los Angeles.

The night of Lana's death

Lana Clarkson arrived at her job at the House of Blues on 2nd of February 2003. She was managing the VIP area that night and she was her typical self, treating every guest kindly and with respect. Phil Spector started his night out somewhere around 07:00 PM by taking his first date for a dinner. He would shortly meet his second date for the evening and would eventually ask his driver to go to the House of Blues as their last stop. He was a well-known figure there and even though the place was crowded, he knew that a table was waiting for him inside.

When Spector approached the VIP area, Lana didn't recognize him. As a matter of fact, she told him: "Madam, you are not allowed to enter." Spector was wearing one of his wigs and Lana had mistaken him for a woman. Lana's friend quickly pulled her to the side and explained that the "madam" was actually Phil Spector. The fact that Lana had no idea who he was shouldn't surprise anyone because, by that time, Spector wasn't a household name. She apologized to him and found Spector a table to sit at. She was a wonderful hostess and Spector noticed it right away. He was blown away by her height and beauty.

Lana's shift ended sometime before two AM and she packed things in order to go home and rest for the night. She exited the House of Blues and went to get her car. The surveillance from the House of Blues would later reveal that Lana was approached by Spector's car as she was leaving at half past two. You can clearly see that she entered the vehicle and drove away with him. Spector invited Lana to his castle in order to have a drink. Lana probably accepted the invitation out of politeness because she learned that Spector was a big name and she didn't want to insult him. Plus, networking is incredibly important in Hollywood.

It is unclear when they arrived at Spector's house but Adriano de Souza, the driver of the car remained parked in front of the mansion. Spector exited the house in the early hours, stood in front of the car with a gun in his hand and said to de Souza: "I think I've killed someone." De Souza was speechless at the moment but he knew he had to call the police. He did hear a loud sound before Spector appeared in front of him but had no idea what happened inside of the house. The driver entered the mansion, found the phone and talked to the 911 operator for a couple of minutes. The police were quickly dispatched to Alhambra and they arrived at the crime scene. They were met by a grisly scene right there in the foyer of the house.

The analysis of the crime scene

When the police showed up at the Spector's house at 05:10 AM, they found Lana's body in a chair near the main entrance. She was slumped back and had a visible gunshot wound in her mouth. Spector who remained in the house was frantic and the detectives noticed that he was intoxicated. The arrest was made immediately and Spector was transported to the police station in order to be interrogated. The remaining police officers continued to investigate the crime scene in order to put the pieces back together and find out what happened in those early morning hours prior to the murder.

The gun was laying on the floor near Lana's body. It was wiped clean and had no fingerprints on it which was very strange, especially since Spector claimed that the shooting was an accident and that Lana decided to take her own life. The police officers were unsure about whose weapon it was. They quickly found a cabinet drawer that was partially open. It contained an empty gun holster that matched the weapon find by Lana's body so it was obvious that the gun belonged to Spector. As a matter of fact, they would later uncover nine more firearms all around the house which indicated that Spector was an avid gun collector.

Back at the station, Spector told the investigators that Lana committed suicide. That story was flawed from the very beginning, especially because the police officers knew that Spector told his driver that he had murdered Lana. The suicide theory was very unlikely and Spector refused to continue talking to them without his lawyer present in the interrogation room.

The detectives were combing through the house and they found proof that Spector tried to clean up the murder scene. A bloody cloth was discovered in a nearby bathroom while Lana's blood was found all around the house. Spector's hands were bloody and he left the marks on door handles and the staircase leading to his bedroom. Investigators followed the trail and discovered Spector's coat hanging in his closet. It had blood speckles on it. They would later confirm that Spector wore it on the night out and was likely in the same coat when he murdered Lana. They collected the clothes and sent everything for blood spatter analysis. It will become one of the main evidence in this case.

Phil Spector was charged with the murder of Lana Clarkson and the bail was set for one million dollars. Spector was shortly released because he had the money and the power. He didn't return to the house right away since it was still investigated by the police. Instead, he hid in a hotel for a week until he got the approval from the authorities. The suicide theory wasn't completely ruled out yet and the police had to investigate every single possible aspect of the story.

Lana's career wasn't going too well at the moment and was stalled due to the accident she had in 2001 when she broke both of her wrists. Her friends did report that she was feeling a bit down back then. However, she recovered and seemed perfectly healthy and happy at the time of the murder. She had no good reason to kill herself that night. Spector would continue talking to the media and friends about his innocence and would mention the suicide theory to everyone. He was heard saying that Lana "kissed the gun" that night which was an appalling quote by someone who was a suspect in this murder. It proved how inconsiderate he was to the family and friends of Lana Clarkson.

It took seven months for the police to completely rule out the possibility of suicide. After a thorough examination of the crime scene and all the evidence, the coroner confirmed that Lana's death was a homicide. Dr. Louis Pena examined Lana's body and came to a conclusion that a bullet cut off her spine through the mouth, leading to the instant death. He would later say that it was difficult to determine whether it was a suicide or a homicide with that fact only but he did take other evidence into the consideration. The crime scene indicated that the death of Lana Clarkson was a homicide and Dr. Pena stood firmly by his decision during the trial.

Phil Spector was charged with murder in November of 2003, exactly nine months after the event. As it was expected, Spector pleaded not guilty and he started getting ready for the big trial. He was a wealthy man that could afford the best defense in the country so he had an excellent team of lawyers behind him. Spector was used to getting what he wanted and he was sure that he couldn't lose in court.

The trial

In the years prior to the trial, Phil Spector made a couple of videos which were uploaded to his official website. They show a hectic Spector trying to defend himself by stating he had no real motive for the murder and continued saying that Lana Clarkson decided to commit suicide that night at his house. He didn't give any good explanation to the fact that Lana apparently found his own gun in a drawer. The videos also show Spector strolling through his home and playing music. They are a rare insight into the odd life of Phil Spector but the clips didn't persuade the public to change their minds.

One of the most memorable quotes from these videos is a segment in which Spector openly defends himself. He said: "I did not have anything to do with her death. She may have accidently taken her own life. She may have purposely taken her own life. She may have been eating the gun while dancing. She may have been doing anything. I don't know why, when, how, or where and in what circumstances she may have taken her own life. Whether she planned to or not." It was clear from Spector's tone of voice and the way he was speaking in these videos that he was doing everything in order to prove his version of the story. But they also indicated that he was mentally unstable.

The trial was just around the corner and Spector started selecting his lawyers. Robert Shapiro, a well-known Hollywood attorney who became famous because he was a part of O.J. Simpson's dream team represented Spector during pretrial hearings but he was soon replaced by Bruce Cutler before the actual trial. Bruce Cutler wasn't an unknown. As a matter of fact, he had close ties to the Gotti family and was John Gotti's lawyer for years. The trial began in March of 2007 and the courtroom was filled with the media. Everything was televised and Spector showed his odd sense of style by wearing outrageous wigs and clothes. He was putting on a show and the public was more focused on the way he looked than the trial itself.

Alan Jackson was leading the prosecution and he was set on bringing justice to Lana and her family. He was aware of the fact that the famous people know their way around justice but he did his best to present this case to the jury and put Spector behind the bars for good. They explored Spector's past to the smallest details and managed to find enough evidence to prove that he was known for pulling guns on people who were close to him, especially on his wives, girlfriends, and lovers.

The prosecution focused their efforts on the evidence collected from the crime scene itself and they started putting the pieces back together in order to paint a clear picture for the jury. They combined the gunshot wound with the blood spatter patterns found on Spector's clothes, as well as an odd positioning of the gun which was found next to Lana. She was right handed but the gun was by her left leg which didn't fit with the suicide theory. The blood drops which were discovered on Spector's white suit indicated that he was right in front of her when the gun was discharged.

She was found in an odd pose and it looked like Lana was trying to move away from whoever was holding the gun in her face. The defense stuck to the suicide theory and called Lana's friends and acquaintances to the stand in order to prove that Lana was depressed at the time of the event. They wanted to show the jury that Lana was a failed actress that was in financial problems and that she was very likely suicidal.

The prosecution had five witnesses and each of them was in a relationship with Spector at some point of time. They told similar stories about Spector who used to threaten them with guns and rifles when he was drunk. He didn't hold his alcohol well and would often get violent if a woman tried to leave. If we take into the consideration that Lana Clarkson had her coat on and the purse was hanging from her shoulder when she was found by the investigators, it looks like the similar thing happened here as well. Unfortunately, the end result was deadly. Spector obviously has a pattern of behavior with women. He has to be in control at all times and threatening someone with a firearm is an effective way to keep them in place.

The trial turned out to be longer than expected, mostly because Spector didn't show any respect to the prosecution and the judge. He switched lawyers at the last moment, firing Bruce Cutler in August of 2007. Linda Kenney Baden became the lead defense lawyer. After each side delivered their final words, the jury retreated in order to deliberate on the final verdict. The prosecution was certain they had a solid case against Spector and that nothing could go wrong. They had the physical evidence, the witnesses, and Spector's strange behavior.

The jury deliberated for twelve days which was a shock to nearly everyone. It was obvious that some members were unsure about the decision so the outcome was a mystery to everyone. They couldn't reach a final conclusion because two jury members simply couldn't be swayed. The result was a hung jury which resulted in the mistrial. The prosecution was shocked but they were more determined than ever to bring Spector to justice. The infamous myth that famous people have a free pass for nearly everything had to be shattered.

The second trial

The prosecution had to move fast and Alan Jackson remained at his position of the head prosecutor. He knew that they had a clear case but they wanted to make sure every single member of the new jury got the evidence right. They quickly filed the papers for the next trial and it was set to begin in October of 2008, a little bit over one year after the mistrial. The same judge was assigned for the second trial as well.

While the defense stuck to their previous tactic in claiming that Lana Clarkson committed suicide in Spector's mansion, the prosecution's goal was to present the evidence as clearly as possible in order to remove any traces of doubt from the jury. Doron Weinberg who was in the defense team asked Spector to tone down his appearance a little bit and avoid changing his hairstyle so often. They tried to make the jury feel sympathetic towards him. The judge banned cameras from the courtroom and the trial wasn't televised.

Spector appeared in front of the jury on 26th of March, 2009 and the case was presented to the selected twelve members. The hearings lasted for nineteen days and they reached the verdict pretty quickly. Only two jurors were in favor of Spector's innocence and they examined each and every testimony closely in order to reach the unanimous verdict. It appears that the jury in the second trial understood the evidence properly and the final decision was made.

Phil Spector was found guilty of murder 13th of April, 2009. An additional sentencing for using a firearm was included. The sentence was nineteen years to life with the possibility of the parole and it was delivered to him in May of the same year. He is currently being held in California Health Care Facility which is a part of California State Prison in Stockton.

Appeals and the aftermath

Spector's attorneys filed for a review of the sentencing in May 2011 but their request was denied. They made a second attempt in December of the same year in front of Supreme Court of the United States stating their defendant's rights were violated. Their story was that judge was openly on the prosecution's side and providing inappropriate comments about the evidence that led to the guilty verdict. The Supreme Court of the United States dismissed the claims after a close examination of the tapes from the trial itself. Everything was recorded and they found no evidence to support these claims.

They repeated the same petition in 2012 but this time it was in Federal District Court. The judges once again took the case seriously. Their review lasted for three years. Even though Spector's lawyers did their best in order to speed up the process, the investigation was thorough and the case was once again dismissed.

Phil Spector is still behind the bars and he won't be eligible for the parole until 2027. He is currently 77 years old and the chances that he would be set free anytime soon are minimal. This particular case had a huge impact on Hollywood as a community. It was a proof that no matter how rich and famous you are, escaping justice is simply impossible. Yes, the trial lasted for years but Lana Clarkson's family and friends can be sure that the right person was held accountable for this heinous crime.

The Murder of Alfalfa

Olivia Watson

Chapter 1

To many, the name Carl Switzer doesn't ring a bell—the name Alfalfa, however, does.

As Alfalfa, the freckle-faced kid with an unmanageable cowlick, Switzer won movie fame in the *Our Gang* comedies of the early 1930s. He later became known to a new generation of children when the Hal Roach films were reissued to television under the title *The Little Rascals*.

Carl Switzer played the iconic character from 1935-1940, and his popularity surpassed many of the other characters. At the time, no one could've foreseen the saddening circumstances that lead to the end of Switzer's life within twenty years of him leaving the show.

In January of 1959, Carl Switzer was shot dead over a financial dispute with an acquaintance. While the news of his death saddened many, the bizarre circumstances—which involved a dog, a bear, and $50—confused most.

Chapter 2

Carl Switzer was born in Paris Illinois to Gladys Shanks and George Switzer on August 7, 1927. He was the youngest of three children, although he was the fourth born in the family. One of Switzer's older brothers had died five years earlier in 1922.

Switzer was destined to be a performer right from the start of his life. Carl and his brother Harold were well-known around area the family resided in for being entertainers. The brothers loved getting a crowd's attention whether they were making up jokes, singing, or playing one of the numerous instruments they taught themselves.

The Switzer family encouraged their sons to practice their talents and perform as often as possible. Like most families of the era, the Switzers were victims of the Great Depression and money was short. Their father, George Switzer, had lost one of his feet in a work accident in the 1920s, which made it difficult for him to find and keep work. The Switzers relied on unconventional ways to make ends meet, including Harold and Carl performing for money at local agricultural fairs and other community events.

In 1934, the Switzer family decided to take a family vacation to visit relatives in California. On this trip, Carl and Harold begged their parents to take them to where they believed all their dreams would come true—the Hal Roach Studio.

At the time, the Hal Roach production company had been making waves in the entertainment community for their series of short films, *Our Gang*. The *Our Gang* films had begun being produced in the 1920s and were incredibly popular with children and families, including the Switzers. In the movie business, *Our Gang* was also considered groundbreaking as the films relied on the talents of the young stars who formed the rag tag yet charming group of talented children. It was also one of the first series to star both black and white children interacting as equals.

For Carl and Harold Switzer, their only dream was to star in the *Our Gang* series. Unlike so many outlandish dreams that comes with childhood, this dream would come true for them.

Carl's parents agreed to take the family on a guided tour of the Hal Roach Studios. At the end of the tour, the family stopped in the Studio's cafeteria, which served both the public and the workers of Hal Roach.

While in the cafeteria, Carl, then six years old, and Harold, then eight years old, saw an opportunity to do what they did best—perform—so the young boys stood up on the tables and began an impromptu song-and-dance routine. Amazingly for the boys, Hal Roach himself was in the cafeteria at the time and saw the show. He was impressed with the boys' singing talent and the way they captivated their audience. After the boys finished their show, Hal Roach approached their parents about having the boys join *Our Gang*. They immediately accepted Roach's offer. The brothers signed their contracts that very day.

Harold and Carl Switzer first appeared as their characters Slim and Alfalfa in the 1935 *Our Gang* short *Beginner's Luck*. Carl, as the goofy freckle-faced boy with the distinct cowlick, stole the show.

By the end of the year, the brother's had appeared in three other short films, but while Harold had been relegated to the background, Carl's character Alfalfa had become a leading role.

At only seven years old, Carl Switzer was living his dream life. He was the successful star of his favorite show and he got to do what he loved to do best—perform. Between 1935 and 1940, Switzer acted in over 60 episodes of *Our Gang*, which was known as *The Little Rascals* after 1938. During this time, he also appeared in a dozen or so unrelated films.

In 1940, Switzer was 13-years-old and had begun to outgrow his boyish charm that made him the iconic character, Alfalfa. He decided to leave Hal Roach Studios and the *Our Gang* squad.

Chapter 3

After leaving *Our Gang*, Switzer still found success as an actor. Even without his straightened cowlick, Switzer was still recognizable as a talented young actor and was in high demand. He appeared in several films in a row including *It's A Wonderful Life* and *Going My Way*.

In the 1950s, Switzer made the switch to the small screen. Between 1952 and 1955, he made six appearances on the *Roy Rogers Show* and guest-starred in an episode of *Science Fiction Theatre*, an American science fiction anthology, as well as guest starring on *The George Burns Show* and the *Gracie Allen Show*.

Carl Switzer's success after Alfalfa was not lifelong, however. Each year Switzer aged he looked less and less like the iconic role that had won him his fame. With movie contracts becoming more difficult to secure, and amid rumors of poor behaviour on set, Switzer stopped being able to land new roles and began to run out of money, forcing him to pause his acting career to find other ways to make money.

Between acting roles, Switzer began to breed and train hunting dogs. He had been hunting since he was a young boy, before his Alfalfa days, growing up in Illinois. There was money in hunting, and Switzer also began leading guided hunting expeditions.

In 1954, Switzer went on a date that had been set up for him by a friend. His date was Diantha Collingwood. An heiress in the world of grain, Collingwood came from the family who owned and operated Collingwood Grain, a company that dominated the grain elevator empire at the time.

Collingwood had moved to California the year before with her mother and sister, who wanted to be an actress. She didn't know a lot of people in the area, and agreed to the date initially only as a way to meet new people and hopefully find a new friend.

Collingwood and Switzer hit it off from the get go though, something that surprised both of them. After only three months of dating, the couple got swept up in their new love and visited Las Vegas, where they were married.

Diantha became pregnant shortly after the couple's wedding, but her family had some growing concerns about whether Carl could adequately provide for their daughter and now grandchild as well. By this time, it was clear that Switzer's remarkable run in the entertainment industry was now over, and breeding dogs didn't come with a hefty salary. Collingwood's family decided to offer the couple a farm near Pretty Prairie, Kansas, to live and work on. It was an opportunity for the couple to make a new, sustainable life together.

The couple moved to their new farm property, which was just West of Wichita, in 1956. Shortly after settling in to the new property, Diantha gave birth to their first child—Justin Collingwood Switzer. However, not all was well with the new family.

Carl had a hard time adjusting to his new life as a farmer and he disliked the distance it put him from the world he had grown up in. After a few months of marriage, the glamour of Carl's childhood life wore off on Diantha, and she grew tired of listening to Carl's stories of the good ole days, which had since morphed into a series of recurring complaints and grievances. Carl had also begun to drink heavily.

Early 1957, Diantha had had enough of Carl's moaning and lack of ambition and kicked him out of the house. Their son was not even a year old yet, and it was made clear to Carl that he would have no place in the child's life. Carl left the farm life behind him in favor of the glamour of California for the second time in his life.

Chapter 4

Carl Switzer's return to California was nowhere near as successful as his initial pilgrimage to the land of his childhood hopes and dreams. Switzer was no longer on the casting radar of many studios and his new drinking habit prevented him from maintaining any form of steady work. He did appear in a few movie roles, but nothing of note. He spent the time he had in between jobs simply making ends meet. He took up a job as a bartender and began leading hunting tours again.

Bars became Switzer's new home during this time in his life. If he wasn't working, he was drinking, dreaming about the old days.

One night in January of 1958, Carl Switzer decided to spend his evening drinking with some friends to help pass the time. Switzer met up with a group of buddies in Studio City, where they spent their evening. After a few good laughs, and a few more good drinks, Switzer decided to call it a night.

Switzer left the bar ahead of his friends and walked across the street to where his car was parked. Just as he was climbing into the driver's side door, a loud crack rang out, splitting the cool night air. The next thing he knew, Switzer was bleeding profusely from his right bicep—he had been shot.

His friends, who were now several yards up the road from him searching for their own ways home, were in shock. They heard the gunshot but hadn't seen who was responsible. All they had seen was a car screeching down the road and their friend laying on the ground, bleeding. They rushed to his side as someone else yelled that they were running inside to call 9-1-1.

Carl Switzer was rushed to the hospital, but his injuries were fairly minor. The bullet hadn't pierced any major arteries so Switzer's blood loss was minimal. After a few stitches and a visit from the local police department, Switzer was released.

Initially, police were fairly confident that they would be able to figure out who had shot Carl Switzer that night. Usually drive-by shootings are difficult to piece together to find out who's responsible, but there were several witnesses on the road at the time that were able to describe the vehicle that sped down the road from the crime. As well, the police figured that it couldn't have been a coincidence that the man shot that night happened to be well-known, both for his acting career and for being a confrontational drunk.

Despite their early hopes, police were never able to identify the assailant. They looked into several leads from a list Switzer provided of who may have wanted him hurt, but none of the leads panned out. As well, they had a hard time identifying witnesses, let alone witnesses who were able to provide accurate statements, and all of Switzer's own friends had been walking away from the crime when it happened so their statements were labelled unreliable.

Later that year, Switzer found himself dealing with the law again, but this time he was on the wrong side. For reasons that are still unclear to many, in December of 1958, Carl Switzer was arrested in Sequoia National Forest when he was caught cutting down fifteen pine trees.

Sequoia National Forest lies in the southern Sierra Nevada mountains in California. It's a popular destination for those who love nature, as the Forest is populated by beautiful, Giant Sequoia trees. The National Forest is a protected area, so understandably no one was happy when Switzer's destruction was discovered. He was arrested on the site and was later sentenced to a year's probation and a $225 fine. Switzer told police he was planning on selling the trees to make some extra pocket cash leading up to the Christmas season. It was his only short foray in the industry.

Within the same year, Switzer had been arrested, shot in the arm, and let go from several jobs. It was clear that his days as a loveable hooligan were over—no one was laughing at his antics now.

Chapter 5

While Carl Switzer's arrest in 1958 was his first time behind bars, it wasn't the first time in his life that his often behaviour got him into trouble.

Offscreen, on the set of *Our Gang*, Switzer's behaviour resembled more a pint-sized Dirty Harry than the boy next door.

"We were children under contract. Even at that young age we understood that what we were doing was expensive for the studio, so we had to do what we were told. Most of us were pretty good kids" Jerry Tucker, who played a rich kid in *The Little Rascals* once said.

Carl Switzer was the exception. For the most part, Switzer did his own thing. When he first joined the cast, he didn't quite fit in with the rest of the children. They had all mostly grown up around California and Los Angeles whereas Switzer's family had been from the hills of Illinois. Switzer once told his new friends that he had never really worn shoes before coming to California.

He had also grown used to getting a lot of attention back at home where he truly was the only star in his neighbourhood. Now, he was surrounded by other talented children who he had to share his spotlight with. Acting out got him the attention he craved. He had always loved an audience.

One of Switzer's most popular forms of acting out was disappearing right before he was needed on set. When the Director called for him, he would be out of sight.

Further, the whole gang of children on set were expected to balance work, play, and studying. They would attend group lessons in between filming. Each child needed to complete at least three hours of lessons a day, which would be interspersed between filming scenes. When a child was needed on set they would leave the class, complete their scene, and return to the group to finish their schoolwork for the day.

When it came time to study, Switzer always put up a fight. He was not a good student. He disliked the group's teacher and often refused to attend his lessons. When he did attend, he was often held late to make up for missed time. Because education for their young stars was required, the studio couldn't refuse the teacher when she said Switzer needed to stay longer at the end of the day, even if it meant delaying filming.

Seventeen years later at a reunion celebration, Carl Switzer swore at his old teacher in front of his former castmates, blaming her for ruining his life and proving that he still held a grudge. Switzer's former costars were not surprised by his behaviour that night. They had seen his bad side from the start.

Switzer was described as a bully on set. He liked to pick on the younger kids, but didn't hold out from bullying the older kids either. He would stomp on his castmates feet and hit them when the adults weren't looking. More often than one would expect, he would carry nails in his pockets and prick any castmate who stood close enough with them.

If things didn't go right for the young star, Switzer would lose his temper. Tantrums were frequent and often started over small problems. Whether he liked them or not, Switzer always let his costars know how he felt about them, and fistfights were never out of the question.

Although he was very abrasive on set, many of his costars still remember him as being a good kid, he was just different. The studio worked hard to make each of the kids feel like equals. Because of his behaviour, Switzer spent a lot of time alone on set. He tried to excuse his antics as just being jokes, but no one was laughing. Even his older brother frequently distanced himself from Carl's behaviour.

Switzer's bully behaviour wasn't reserved for only the kids on set either. On one occasion, Switzer threw a lit firecracker at Kenneth Smith's, or *Waldo's*, father. Switzer ran off as the firecracker exploded right behind the man's back.

On another occasion, Switzer was struggling with a line when a cameraman, who was anxious to break for lunch, told him to just get it right. Switzer responded by spending his lunch break chewing a wad of gum, which he then stuck into the gears of the man's camera. No one was able to work after lunch that day, but the cameraman.

One particular stunt of Switzer stands out above the rest in his castmates' memories: the time he urinated on one of the set lights. While this stunt sounds like the harmless behaviour of an attention-craving child, it was actually quite dangerous. The set lights get really hot when they're in use, and no one knew what Switzer had done.

When the crew turned on the lights everything seemed fine until they heated up. Without warning, the lightbulbs Switzer had urinated on burst, filling the air with a fine dust of shattered glass, chemicals from the filaments, and a foul urine stench. Some of the crew were cut up by the exploding lightbulbs and the studio was unusable for the rest of the day due to the smell.

It's hard to believe that Switzer could have made any friends while working on *Our Gang* with these kinds of stunts, but he did. His castmates put up with his behaviour because they understood he had had a different kind of upbringing then them. They also knew that Switzer cared a lot about the show and making them all successful, even if he didn't act that way all of the time. Most of all though, when Switzer did make friends with some of his costars, he made a great friend.

"If Carl liked you, and was your friend, he loved you. There was no inbetween with him. When Carl loved you, he really loved you. He was the best friend you could've ever hoped for," Tommy Bond, who played *Butch* has said of his childhood friend.

On the set of *Our Gang*, Bond and Switzer were very close. They played rivals on the show, which many people attribute to the reason they got along so well—they could never replace each other on the show, so there was no rivalry between them.

As an adult, Switzer had a more difficult time maintaining friendships except with those who were very close to the former child actor. Switzer's alcoholism often drew acquaintances away, they never got to meet the real Carl. One such poor acquaintanceship eventually lead to Switzer's death.

Chapter 6

After being arrested in late 1958 at the Sequoia National Forest, things were looking rough for Carl Switzer. It had been some time since he landed an acting job, and he was having to live off odd jobs here and there. His main gig was still leading hunting expeditions, but he was struggling even with this.

Before the end of the year, though, things began to look up. Switzer, then 31, was given a supporting role in the film *The Defiant Ones*. The film was shaping up to be quite popular, and many critics thought the movie would be Switzer's gateway back into the acting world as an adult.

While Switzer was excited by the prospects of being a star again, he still needed to earn a living while the movie was being finished in post-production. Early January of 1959, Switzer was gearing up to lead a bear hunting party into the California forests. He borrowed a hunting dog from his acquaintance Moses "Bud" Stiltz and planned to head out the next day.

Before he even got the dog to his house though, it caught a scent in the street and took off. Switzer spent hours looking for the animal but was unsuccessful in finding the fugitive hound. Switzer couldn't afford to replace the dog, so he posted a reward of $35 for its safe return.

A few days later, a man called Switzer to claim the money. Switzer was elated and instructed the man to deliver the dog to the bar where Switzer was also working at the time. After the dog was safely back in Switzer's possession he gave the man the reward money and the two got to chatting. When the man left the bar, Switzer was still so happy the dog was back that he offered to pay the man's $15 tab.

When Switzer returned the dog to Stiltz, Stiltz considered the two men even. All was well between them until an incident that occurred several weeks later.

On January 21, 1959, Carl Switzer was out drinking with friends. Before the end of the night, Switzer had run out of money, but wasn't ready to quit drinking yet. Suddenly, he thought of a place he could get more money—from Moses Stiltz.

In his drunken stupor, Switzer decided that Stiltz should pay him back the $50 he spent getting his dog back, despite the fact that it was his own fault the dog had run away. It didn't matter to him at the time; all that mattered to him was making some quick cash for some quick drinks.

Shortly before 7:00p.m., Switzer arrived at Rita Corrigan's home in Mission hills, where Stiltz was staying, along with his drinking buddy Jack Piott. The pair demanded to be let in, and when Stiltz complied, Switzer immediately ordered Stiltz to repay him the money or there would be trouble.

Stiltz refused to pay Switzer back. Switzer had been at fault for losing the dog in the first place and had also been the one to offer a reward for its return. The two began physically fighting, during which time Switzer threw a glass-domed clock at Stiltz. The clock struck the man in the face, causing him to bleed from his left eye.

It's at this point in the story that the details become unclear.

According to Stiltz, after Switzer threw the clock at him, Switzer pulled out a switch knife and told him that if he didn't pay up, he was going to kill him. Stiltz told him he was going to his room to grab the money, but returned instead with his .38-caliber revolver. Switzer charged Stiltz and grabbed his revolver, which caused a shot to be fired into the ceiling. Switzer then allegedly pulled the knife to Stiltz's neck and threatened again to kill him. In reply, Stiltz pulled the trigger and shot him in the stomach.

According to Stiltz, he had acted in self-defense. He had not wanted to kill the man and would not have had Switzer put the knife down and walked away. When asked to confirm Stiltz's story, Jack Piott, Switzer friend, said he was too shocked by his friend dying to recall specifics.

Moses Stiltz was never charged for the crime.

Carl Switzer's family, friends, and several castmates from *Our Gang* have since spoken to the media regarding the incident. Although they were all too familiar with Switzer's antics and violent temper, none of them believe that Switzer would have ever threatened someone with a knife. Even at his worst, it just wasn't in his spirit.

Unfortunately, there was too little evidence at the scene of the fight to either dispute or corroborate Stiltz's story. There was clear evidence of a struggle, and there was a knife found under Switzer's body, but the knife blade was shut, leaving many people to believe it was placed under his body after Switzer died.

We may never know the truth behind the unnecessary death of Carl Switzer, but Switzer's memory lives on in those who loved him, and those he loved fiercely in return. To many, Switzer will always live on as the young freckled-faced Alfalfa—the boy with the untamable cowlick and famously off-key singing. Those were Switzer's glory days, the happiest days he ever had. He had lived his dreams. And for those dreams he will always be remembered.

THE MURDER OF KARYN KUPCINET

OLIVIA WATSON

Chapter 1

In the latter half of 1963, Karyn Kupcinet was living in Hollywood while pursuing her one true dream: to become a famous starlet. She was constantly on the lookout for the role that would land her her big break. From an outsider's perspective, Kupcinet was well-equipped for and well on her way to stardom. Her life had all the ingredients: she had a wealthy, well-known father, an actor boyfriend whose career was gaining steam, and dark sultry looks that many would have died for. However, behind the scenes, not all was as it seemed.

In reality, Kupcinet's life was on a dramatic downward spiral in the latter half of 1963. Her relationship with her boyfriend, Andrew Prine, was strained at best and her mental health was deteriorating since undergoing an illegal abortion in July of that year. On November 28, 1963, she was dead.

Karyn Kupcinet's life began in a much-less dramatic manner than in which it was taken though. Karyn Kupcinet was born on March 6, 1941 in Chicago. As a young child, she acquired the nickname "Cookie." That was what her parents liked to call her, so was so sweet she'd give you a toothache.

Karyn did not get her sweet side from her mother though. Esther Kupcinet was often described as not caring about anyone unless they were famous. It was no surprise when she began grooming her young daughter to become an actress. She was from the Gold Coast in Chicago, a picturesque neighborhood that's home to Chicago's most affluent residents. Esther herself was a failed wannabe-dancer who imparted a love of the fame-filled lifestyle into her young daughter.

Her mother, Esther Kupcinet, would be the one to encourage Karyn to pursue acting as a career later in her life, but it would be her father who gave her the means to do so. Karyn's father was Irv Kupcinet, was a well-known and well-respected newspaper columnist for the *Chicago Sun-Times* who also worked as a television talk-show host and radio personality. To many in Chicago, he was known simply, but immediately, as "Kup."

Earlier in his life, Kupcinet was a Philadelphia Eagle. Kupcinet joined the NFL team after playing for the University of North Dakota. He was signed in 1935, and many thought he had a long career ahead of him playing for the team. Unfortunately, after playing only part of his first season, Kupcinet sustained a serious shoulder injury which benched him for the remainder of the season. After surgery Kupcinet was told that his shoulder would never fully recover, so Irv retired from his short run in the NFL.

After retiring from the NFL, Irv Kupcinet decided to combine his love and knowledge of sports with another passion of his that he developed in high school—reporting. Kupcinet took a job as a sports writer for the *Chicago Daily Times*. Kupcinet flourished at the job, and soon began writing about more than just sports. In 1948, Kupcinet was given his own column, *Kup's Column*, which chronicled the nightlife and celebrity scene of Chicago.

Kupcinet's success with the *Chicago Daily Times* filtered through many aspects of his career. The paper had built up his fame, and Kupcinet was now well-known in Chicago. In 1952, Kupcinet translated his fame for television when he landed his own talk show. Later, he was part of a group of talented talk show hosts who replaced Steve Allen on *The Tonight Show*.

By the time Kupcinet launched his talk show in 1952, he was almost a household name in Chicago. Thirty-four years and 15 Emmy Awards later, Kupcinet was a household name across America.

In 1957, Irv's daughter, Karyn Kupcinet, was in high school. She was 16 years old and starting to think about her future for the first time. She knew she wanted to be in the spotlight, she was a natural beauty and she admired her father's fame. Her mother suggested she pursue acting and Karyn loved the idea. She had participated in school plays since she was thirteen but had never thought of pursuing acting as a career before. Karyn soon discovered that having a father with his own television show syndicated on over 70 stations across America opened a lot of doors in Hollywood.

Chapter 2

During high school, Karyn Kupcinet decided she wanted to become a famous actress. She spent her senior year applying to arts colleges across the country and was accepted to Pine Manor College. After graduation, Kupcinet left her hometown and family for Boston, determined to hone her acting skills at the liberal arts college.

Kupcinet's time at Pine Manor was short-lived though. In fact, the young starlet-to-be studied in Boston for only a single semester before packing back up and moving to New York City. In New York, Kupcinet began studying at the Actors Studio, a membership organization for those who are determined to succeed in the world of show business.

Through connections she made at the Actors Studio, and through connections with producers she acquired through her father, Karyn landed her first professional role in the 1961 Jerry Lewis film *The Ladies Man*. In her first role, Kupcinet played a bit part as a young lady in a Hollywood boardinghouse alongside dozens of other young starlet wannabes.

Amongst the crowd of young ladies, Kupcinet managed to stand out. The same year, she appeared in two episodes of *Hawaiian Eye*, an episode of *The Andy Griffith Show*, and an episode of *The Donna Reed Show*.

Kupcinet was getting positive reviews for her roles, and went on to guest star in many other popular television shows. In 1962 she was awarded roles in *The Red Skeleton Show*, and *G.E. True*.

As well as these guest roles, Kupcinet also landed her first starring role in 1962 on the primetime series *Mrs. G. Goes to College*, which was later retitled *The Gertrude Berg Show* for its run. The premise of *The Gertrude Berg Show* was that a middle-aged Jewish widow enrolls in a college as a freshman after her children are all grown up. While at college, she interacts with a variety of younger students and her Cambridge University exchange professor, who was played by Cedric Hardwicke.

Kupcinet played the role of Carol, a classmate of Mrs. G. who dated her good friend Joe Caldwell, who was played by Skip Ward. Kupcinet's character had little dialogue, but her dark, sultry looks stood out from the background.

In 1962, Kupcinet also completed one of her first interviews as an actress on the rise. She was interviewed by the *Los Angeles Times* to help promote *Mrs. G. Goes to College*. This interview was supposed to promote her profile as a hirable, talented actress as well, but many instead thought it provided insight into the extreme pressure the young starlet was facing.

During the interview, Kupcinet spoke highly of her cast mates and the show, but had a difficult time talking about her own involvement in the program. When the questions turned to herself, Kupcinet talked exclusively about food and her body weight.

Despite facing an inner pressure, Kupcinet won more acting roles, which she was praised for. After *Mrs. G. Goes to College* finished its short run, Kupcinet appeared in *The Wide Country,* and *Going My Way.* While her role in these shows were short, her work on *The Wide Country* garnered the attention of one person in particular—the show's star Andrew Prine.

Andrew Prine was an actor who came to Hollywood from Florida in 1957 when he first appeared in a single episode of *U.S. Steel Hour.* By 1962, Prine had hit it big. In the same year, Prine was cast in both the Academy Award-nominated film, *The Miracle Worker,* as Helen Keller's older brother, and in the lead role of the NBC series *The Wide Country.*

The Wide Country was an American Western drama about two brothers who worked in the travelling rodeo circuit. The older brother Mitch, played by Earl Holliman, warns his brother about the dangers of following in his own footsteps in the bronco riding world, but Prine's character, Andy, refuses to listen.

In December of 1962, Andrew Prine crossed Karyn Kupcinet's path when she guest starred on *The Wide Country*. On screen, their characters never interacted, but off screen, the pair couldn't keep their eyes, or their hands, off one another.

The two rising stars began dating each other, and on paper they seemed to be a match made in heaven. They were both young, attractive, and chasing stardom. In reality, however, the relationship was very strained.

Once the puppy love phase of their relationship passed, Prine was hesitant to make the relationship exclusive. They were both busy workers with packed schedules and they were young. Prine had just begun to make his mark in Hollywood, and didn't want to settle down or dedicate too much of his time to another person. Most of all, though, Prine was worried that Kupcinet would be a mar on his good reputation.

Although she was receiving good review for her work, Kupcinet was beginning to crumble under the enormous pressure she felt to follow in her father's footsteps of success. Kupcinet began abusing diet pills in 1961. Diet pills in the 1960s were not the same as they are today. Little was known about the properties of many ingredients, so the FDA often approved substances that were not safe for consumption.

One of the most popular diet pills at the time was Obetrol, which was approved by the FDA on January 19, 1960. Obetrol was marketed as a way to lose and control a person's weight. It was a popular drug at the time, and many believed that it was effective in helping them feel more energetic and lose weight quicker, which is not surprising as it was a formulation of three amphetamine mixed salts, including methamphetamine.

Along with her addiction to diet pills, Kupcinet also began abusing prescription drugs in the early 1960s. This combination proved too much for Kupcinet, who began to deteriorate. Despite coming from a wealthy family who were happy to support the young star, Kupcinet began shoplifting from popular stores and was arrested in 1963 for stealing two books, a sweater, and a pair of capris pants. Andrew Prine was mortified by Kupcinet's arrest, worried about how it would reflect on him through their connection.

By August of 1963, Karyn Kupcinet's relationship with Andrew Prine was all but over. In the previous month, Kupcinet underwent an illegal abortion in Tijuana after becoming pregnant with Prine's child. Prine had encouraged Kupcinet to undergo the procedure to protect both of their reputations and because he had no intention of marrying Kupcinet as she had hoped.

After the procedure, Prine declared their relationship over and began dating other women, but Kupcinet wasn't about to let her first love end quite yet.

Chapter 3

By the latter half of 1963, Karyn Kupcinet had lost her touch on reality. Her first love, Andrew Prine, had finally severed all ties to the young starlet due to her addiction to prescription and diet pills, but she wasn't ready to let go. Kupcinet began stalking Prine at his home, and would write about these experiences in her diary.

July 30th read, *Andy with Anna. Me watched from hedge. Awful. Nightmares.*

August 20th followed, *So humiliated by Andy's lack of interest.*

On October 29th she wrote, *Andy acting ugly. Complete indifference. Scene at his house. I'm hysterical.*

While these short messages tell a foreboding tale, the worst entries came from November.

On the 4th, after hiding in Prine's attic, she wrote *Wish I were dead,* and 24 days later on November 28, 1963, she was.

Months before her death, though, Kupcinet put a great deal of effort into making her Prine believe that her life, and his, were in great danger.

Along with stalking Prine and his new girlfriends at his house, Kupcinet began sending letters to Prine. But these were no ordinary letters. Kupcinet would put together threatening and profanity-filled hate mail composed of words cut from magazines. She sent these letters anonymously to Prine, sometimes skipping the post and dropping them off right on his doorstep.

But Prine suspected Kupcinet was behind these letters, so he confronted her. Luckily for her, Kupcinet had thought ahead and composed several similar letters to herself, claiming they had also been anonymously sent to her. She was hoping this would inspire a desire to protect in Prine, but he remained wary of his unstable ex.

Prine always remembered these startling letters. After Kupcinet's death, he had police examine the letters to see if they could determine who had sent them. The answer was no surprise to him. Investigators were able to find Kupcinet's fingerprints all over them, including on the sticky side of the scotch tape used to secure the frightening messages to the paper.

On the night of November 28, 1963, Kupcinet had dinner with her close friends Mark Goddard and his wife Marcia Rogers Goddard at their Beverly Hills House. She was an hour late for dinner, arriving at 7:30p.m. when the dinner had begun at 6:30p.m. The Goddard's later told police that Kupcinet was surprised they had waited for her to eat, and she hardly touched her food throughout the meal.

This was normal for Kupcinet though, who had struggled with body issues and the pressure to stay thin since high school. What wasn't normal, however, was the state Kupcinet was in. Marcia Goddard told authorities that that night Kupcinet acted very strangely during their last meal together. Her lips seemed numb and her voice sounded funny. She moved her head at odd angles and her pupils were incredibly small.

Mark Goddard had confronted Kupcinet about this odd behaviour during the meal, accusing her of being high. Kupcinet immediately began to cry and deny being on any substances and instead blamed her behaviour on the unsubstantiated claim that she had found an abandoned baby on her doorstep earlier that day.

An hour after she arrived, Kupcinet left the Goddard's house in a taxi cab headed home. She promised to call her friends the next day when she was feeling better. After arriving home, she was visited by two friends of hers, Edward Rubin and Robert Hathaway, who also happened to be neighbors and close friends with her ex-boyfriend.

According to Hathaway and Rubin, the three friends watched TV and had coffee with Kupcinet before she fell asleep beside them on the couch. They woke her up and helped her get to her bedroom. After this, the men said they turned the TV off, locked the doors, and left around 11:15p.m.

The men then headed over to Robert Hathaway's house where they were joined by Andrew Prine himself. The three friends chatted and watched TV until 3:00a.m.

The next day, the Goddard's waited for Karyn Kupcinet's call, but it never came. They figured she must have either forgotten or was too embarrassed about her behaviour to check in so they waited a couple of days. They hardly went half a week without hearing from the young woman, so they figured she would call soon enough.

On the third day with no call, the Goddard's began to panic, so they decided to visit Kupcinet's West Hollywood apartment to make sure she was okay. What they found shocked them both, and would forever remain in their memories.

Chapter 4

November 30, 1963. West Hollywood. It's been three days since Mark and Marcia sent Karyn Kupcinet home from their dinner party after her strange behaviour. That night, Kupcinet had promised to call the couple the next morning to check in, but she never did. Mark now feared that his good friend had died from a drug overdose.

The couple arrived at Kupcinet's West Hollywood apartment around noon. They walked through the unlocked front door and found a horrific sight—Karyn Kupcinet was lying face-down on the couch. She was completely nude.

The Goddard's immediately contacted the police, who began investigating immediately. Initially, it looked like the Goddard's suspicions had been true, that Kupcinet had overdosed on the number of drugs she had been abusing over the course of the last few years. Investigators found prescriptions and numerous bottles of Desoxyn, Miltown, Amvicel, Thyroid extract and Modaline strewn around Kupcinet's bathroom.

There was other evidence in the apartment that Kupcinet may have taken her own life; the strongest piece of evidence they found to support this was a cryptic note found in her bedroom which reflected her emotions regarding her life, her parents, her self-image, and her boyfriend.

This note was written in a haphazard fashion, a similar style to her diary entries. One of the most poignant pieces of the note read:

I'm no good. I'm not really that pretty. My figure's fat and will never be the way my mother wants it. Why must I be so alone. What's the use of living with nothing to believe it?

Clearly, Kupcinet was not in a good mental state in the months leading up to her death, and this note proved that without a doubt.

Also at the scene, investigators realized that Kupcinet had not died that day. In fact, she had been dead for several days. Her body had begun decomposing and there was evidence that flies had found Kupcinet first, laying eggs in her scalp. None of the eggs had hatched yet.

Additionally, there was some evidence of distress around Kupcinet's living room. The TV was on, but the volume was turned almost all the way down. Nearby the couch was a metal coffee pot and a brandy glass full of cigarette butts that had been overturned on the floor. A coffee cup sat on a side table across a room next to a pile of matches that had been shredded and cut up by scissors.

In Kupcinet's bedroom, investigators found that all of her dresser drawers were opened and most of the contents had been flung across the room.

Because it was clear that Kupcinet's mental health was unstable leading up to her death, police weren't sure if the mess they found in the apartment was a sign that a struggle had occurred or simply another indication of Kupcinet's mental distress. Form the scene alone, they were unable to determine whether Kupcinet had died from an attack, an accident, or an unintentional suicide.

Kupcinet's body was transferred to a nearby coroner. Sidney Korshak, a Los Angeles based lawyer that had been friends with the Kupcinet family for years, officially identified her body the next day. Shortly after Kupcinet was officially identified, an autopsy was performed on her corpse. The results of which shocked everyone in the case.

After the coroner completed the autopsy, it was determined that Karyn Kupcinet had in fact been murdered. According to the coroner, she had been dead for two days, and her cause of death was manual strangulation due to injuries on her neck that included a compression fracture to the left side of her hyoid bone with deep soft tissue hemorrhages in her neck, thyroid gland, and larynx.

After the autopsy, Kupcinet's body was returned to her hometown, Chicago, where she was laid to rest just outside of the city in Skokie, Illinois. While over 500 people attended her funeral, Andrew Prine did not.

After Karyn was laid to rest, the Kupcinet family was ready for investigators to discover who had murdered their beloved daughter so they could begin to heal. They had no idea at the time the media frenzy that would surround their daughter's murder later, or that the mystery of her death would never be officially solved.

Chapter 5

Karyn Kupcinet's death was initially highly publicized in the Los Angeles media, especially when it was discovered that another up-and-coming star was the main suspect—Andrew Prine. The LAPD believed that Prine was one of the only people who would have had a motive to kill Kupcinet. If she died, he would no longer be haunted by his ex-girlfriend who refused to let him forget her. As well, Prine strongly suspected that Kupcinet had been behind the threatening letters that tormented him.

As well, Prine had spoken to Kupcinet over the phone several times the day before she died, arguing, which was overheard by multiple sources. Prine had an airtight alibi for the night that Kupcinet was killed, but his friends, Robert Hathaway and Edward Rubin, had admitted to spending time with Kupcinet the night she was killed. The pair had told police that they left Kupcinet's apartment that night around 11:30p.m., but the only witness who could corroborate this was Andrew Prine himself.

Unfortunately, Prine, Hathaway, and Rubin had all admitted to being in Kupcinet's apartment shortly before her death, police were forced to accredit all physical evidence of them in the apartment to other times. They found no physical evidence that could directly tie either of the three men to Kupcinet at the time of her death.

The LAPD, along with Kupcinet's family, was pretty sure the three men were responsible for Karyn's death, but pretty sure doesn't stand up in a court of law. None of the men ever faced charges in the crime.

With no exciting breaks in the case, Karyn Kupcinet's murder quickly fell out of the newspapers in Los Angeles and out of the minds of its residents. It wasn't until 1967 that Kupcinet's story was thought of by many outside of her own family.

In 1967, Penn Jones Jr., a researcher with a love of conspiracy theories, self-published the book *Forgive My Grief II*, which attempted to present a set of facts as evidence that the JFK assassination hadn't happened the way the media and the government had claimed.

John F. Kennedy was assassinated the day before Kupcinet died. According to Jones, who cited an Associated Press story, an unidentified woman had called her local operator twenty minutes before the assassination of the President, warning of the impending attack. Jones believed that the unidentified woman was Karyn Kupcinet.

Jones cited as proof the fact that the call had come from California, and that Kupcinet's murder could have been connected to her spilling a deadly secret. Karyn, Jones claimed, heard about the assassination from her father, Irv Kupcinet, who allegedly had been told by Jack Ruby, Oswald's killer, whom Irv had met in the 1940s.

Irv Kupcinet continued to deny that he or his daughter had any knowledge of the President's assassination before the rest of America right up until his own death in 2003. Kupcinet wrote about his daughter in *Kup's Column*. In 1992, NBC's *Today Show* ran a segment on mysterious deaths that occurred after JFK's assassination, including Karyn's death. Irv again spoke out against the idea that Karyn had any role in the story surrounding the assassination. He insisted again that both his family and the LAPD knew exactly who had been responsible for her death—Andrew Prine, Robert Hathaway, and Edward Rubin—there just wasn't, nor would there ever be, enough evidence to prove it to a court.

When Irv Kupcinet passed away on November 10, 2003, He was laid to rest next to his daughter and wife, who passed away in 2001. Irv's death marked the end of an era to many Chicagoans, just as it put an end to the investigation into Karyn Kupcinet's death.

In her quest to be seen on every silver screen, Karyn Kupcinet lost sight of herself. Striving to be skinny, the young starlet abused her mind and body excess amounts of prescription and diet pills. When her mind went, so did her chances of finding love and happiness, no matter how hard she tried to maintain it.

Karyn Kupcinet's final appearance on television came a year after her death in 1964. Kupcinet had guest starred on an episode of *Perry Mason*, which had been in post-production at the time of her death and the following year. To many who saw her performance, it seemed the young beauty was just beginning her rise to fame, but she was already gone, taken from the world many years too early.

CHRISTA HELM : THE MURDER OF A HOLLYWOOD STARLET

JESSI DILLARD

Disco's Black Dahlia

"I am in way over my head here," Christa Helm wrote in a postcard to a friend, shortly before her body was found on a street in West Hollywood in 1977, stabbed and bludgeoned to death. "I'm into something I can't get out of."

Tall, blonde, and beautiful, Helm never really made it as an actress – despite leaving her home and a new baby to pursue her career in the movies. However, Helm was touted as the "ultimate party girl," and was a known fixture at parties and bedrooms throughout the Hollywood Hills. Her list of conquests included names like Warren Beatty, Joe Namath, Mick Jagger, and the Shah of Iran – and details of these trysts were recorded in Helm's diary, complete with a rating system to evaluate the bedroom skills of these famous men.

When Helm's body was found, police found the diary missing, as well as the tapes Helm had secretly recorded of her sexual encounters. The suspicion was that Helm had been murdered for what she knew, and may have been extorting the celebrities and politicians that she'd bedded. However, the case has remained unsolved, and to this day, no one really knows what exactly happened to the actress known as Christa Helm.

A troubled past

In November, 1949, Harry and Dolores Wohlfeil welcomed their first of three daughters – Sandra Lynn Wohlfeil, who would grow up to go by the name Christa Helm. Three years after Helm was born, her parents divorced. While Harry went on to remarry and have another two children, Dolores descended into alcoholism and entered into a long series of abusive relationships with a number of violent boyfriends.

According to Helm's daughter Nicole, "many of these guys sexually molested my mother, as well as her younger sisters." Nicole said her grandmother, Dolores, was obviously a "tortured soul" who for many years refused to even recognize that the abuse was taking place. Eventually, Nicole added, Helm and her sisters were saved from the "harrowing home life" they had with Dolores, and went to live with their father and his new wife.

As if her difficult family situation wasn't stressful enough, Helm was plagued by a chronic health condition that usually kept her confined to a bulky, uncomfortable back brace. Nicole said Helm and her two sisters all suffered skeletal problems as a result of Dolores' use of diet pills throughout her life – even during her pregnancies.

Thanks to the brace and the countless sexual abuses she endured, Helm's self-esteem suffered, and by her mid-teens, she was acting out with wild, reckless behaviour. Her rebellious attitude and brash personality attracted her plenty of attention from men, though – as did her honey-brown eyes and beautiful blonde hair.

When she was only 16, Helm fell in love for the first time. Gary Clements was a decade older, and rumored to have connections to the mob in Milwaukee. She got pregnant after only a few weeks, leading to a shotgun wedding in Chicago. However, once Nicole was born, the relationship didn't last – according to Nicole, her father "just vanished one day."

"He kind of disappeared from our lives some time after my christening," she said. "I was told that Mom looked high and low for him and that she couldn't find him. My father never did come back. A few months later, Mom was told by someone that he had died in a motorcycle accident in Florida, but she was never sure if that was true."

From humble beginnings

To make ends meet after her daughter was born, Helm found a job working as a waitress at an Italian restaurant on Milwaukee's East Side. Travato's was reportedly run by the syndicate, but 17-year-old Helm needed a way to bring in some money to support herself and her child. She quickly befriended another waitress, 23-year-old Diane Mitchell. Mitchell still thinks of Helm with fondness, admitting that she "liked her instantly."

"She was down-to-earth and gregarious, as well as very pretty. You wanted to be around (Helm), you know?" Mitchell recalled. "She did what the rest of us only thought about doing."

The women bonded over motherhood, since Mitchell was, at that time, in the middle of a divorce and raising a daughter of her own. Kellena was approximately the same age as Nicole. According to Mitchell, Helm still talked about Clements all the time, and she believed he was "the love of her life."

But Helm was never without suitors. She started seeing a college student named Rolf Siefert while she was working with Mitchell, but not exclusively – the attention she attracted as a result of her bold personality and gorgeous appearance meant Helm could have virtually any man she wanted.

After a time, Helm and Mitchell decided to get an apartment together, a two-bedroom suite located just a few blocks from the restaurant. Nicole and Kellena were staying with their grandmothers, but Mitchell said they would often have them over on weekends. According to Mitchell, Helm invited other people over on the weekends, too – including people she "barely knew."

"I was concerned and told her that it wasn't safe to invite total strangers over to our place like that, but she would just laugh at me. She said it was fine and that I worried too much," Mitchell said. "Lucky thing, most of the people she befriended were fine. There were a couple of strange guys, but, you know, that was (Helm). She didn't seem to be afraid of very much, if anything."

Mitchell added that during that time, Helm wasn't much of a drinker, but did smoke marijuana on occasion – when it was available. She didn't use any other drugs, Mitchell admitted.

Helm's dreams of Hollywood stardom started when she, Mitchell, and two other waitresses were invited by their boss to attend a show at the Playboy Club in Lake Geneva, Wisconsin. The show featured a performance by Gidget star James Darren, and the girls were lucky enough to meet the handsome singer and actor after the show.

"He sat down with us at our table and we were thrilled," Mitchell remembered. "We decided right then and there that we wanted to be Playboy bunnies."

Mitchell and Helm decided to pursue positions at the Chicago club, which was larger than the Playboy Club in Lake Geneva. After the girls were hired "on the spot," Mitchell said they returned several days later for their "bunny fittings," where they were given a tour of the dorm where they would be living and training in both food and drink service.

However, when they returned, Mitchell said her mother "threw a monkey wrench" into the plan and refused to care for her daughter, Kellena, while Mitchell was away working in Chicago.

"I was devastated, as was (Helm)," Mitchell said. "I told her to go to Chicago without me, but she said she didn't want to go alone, so neither of us ever became Playboy bunnies."

When Helm turned 21, the girls decided to leave their daughters in the care of a friend's mother in Virginia so they could move to New York and pursue modeling careers. According to Mitchell, the girls had "no reservations" about having their children stay with Mrs. Gertrude Baker, who Mitchell said was "very nice."

Helm and Mitchell found themselves a room at the local YWCA and started scouring the newspapers to set up modeling interviews. It was a frustrating process, though, since the girls were quite unprepared – with no portfolios, no experience, and no money to fall back on.

"Every newspaper ad was either for straight porno or lesbian-oriented photo shoots," Mitchell admitted. "It was extremely seedy and we got very discouraged."

Eventually, though, the girls managed to find jobs as waitresses. While working at The Gaslight Club, Helm started to date singer Lesley Gore's fiancé before meeting Buffalo Bills football player Ray

Abbruzzese. After dating Abbruzzese for some time, Helm decided to move in with him – and Mitchell decided to pack up and head back home.

"I got tired of living in New York, so I went back to Vermont, picked up my daughter at Mrs. Baker's house, and returned to Milwaukee," Mitchell said. "(Helm) and I kept in touch, and she told me she had begun taking singing and acting lessons at the Gene Frankel Workshop in Manhattan."

A star in the making

Less than a year later, Helm and Abbruzzese's relationship had come to an end, and in 1971 Helm began to date Stuart Duncan, a wealthy Broadway producer who was apparently the primary heir to the fortune of the Lea & Perrin Worcestershire Sauce company.

Helm's modeling career had finally begun to take off, and she began booking regular jobs as a New York fashion model – earning enough to pay for a luxury apartment and even a brand-new Corvette. Duncan persuaded Helm to make a financial investment in his latest stage project, an original, religious musical production that eventually became the show *Godspell*. The production went on to become a huge Broadway hit, netting Helm a sizeable return.

By 1972, Helm was splitting her time between her apartment in the city and a sprawling beachfront home in the beautiful Hamptons of Long Island, where she rubbed shoulders with plenty of celebrities. According to Mitchell, the house was a gift from Duncan, "a token of how much he loved her."

Mitchell recalled visiting Helm at her new house, noting that her long-time friend was finally "living her dream." Helm showed off her recently enlarged breasts and told Mitchell that she was using a new name – acting on the advice of an astrologer. To Mitchell, these were just more examples of Helm's "outrageous" personality.

"I did notice that she had become a bit jaded, but I guess it just went with the territory," Mitchell said, adding that Helm had also started using illegal drugs by this time.

Only 23-years-old, Helm started enhancing her already beautiful appearance with a number of other cosmetic procedures. She also paid to correct her daughter Nicole's eyes – which, according to Mitchell, had been crossed since birth.

Helm wasn't just spending her time with her old friends, though. In New York, she'd made plenty of new acquaintances including Jeremiah Newton, who now works as the Film, Television, and Video Industry Liaison for New York University's Tisch School for the Arts in Manhattan. In the 1970s, though, Newton described himself as a "relentless pub crawler," who frequently visited the Stonewall Inn – a legendary Greenwich Village venue that went on to serve as a landmark for the growing gay pride movement.

Helm was introduced to Newton through their mutual friends Candy Darling and Lennie Barin – both well-known mavericks that freewheeled through New York in the 1970s. Darling, a transsexual friend of Andy Warhol's, lives on in Lou Reed's "Take a Walk on the Wild Side," and Barin was a costume designer who was as known throughout New York City for his flamboyant personality as for his design work.

"Back then, (Helm) was close to both (Barin) and Darling, and while she and I weren't what I would call best friends, she was definitely part of our group," Newton recalled. "I thought that (Helm) was beautiful and an extremely nice person."

Newton remembers Helm's "gorgeous, creamy skin," as well as her beautiful hair and golden skin. He said she'd already had a considerable amount of plastic surgery by that point – including an operation to lengthen her legs, which he said he'd heard had been "quite difficult."

"(Helm) was a straight-shooting, no-nonsense type of person, at least that's how I perceived her to be," Newton added. "She was a fascinating girl."

He also recalled Helm's wealth. When he knew her, he said Helm was living in a seven-room duplex in the East 30s that she called "Merlin's Magical Den." The beautiful apartment was outfitted with an extravagant stereo system, plush white furniture, and an expensive display of crystal figures that Newton remembers quite vividly.

"I was told (Helm) was independently wealthy," Newton said, although a more likely theory is that in those years, Helm received financial support from a number of wealthy male benefactors. "It was understood in our group that she was involved as a major investor in the play *Godspell*, and that she had a lot of money."

Taking the next step

The success of *Godspell*, in fact, encouraged Duncan to pursue production in another medium – film. *Let's Go For Broke* would be Duncan's first independent film, and plans were made to shoot in Haiti in the summer of 1973. The location was selected to help keep the film under budget, but posed considerable additional challenges when it came to creatively addressing government restrictions, and keeping the cast and crew working through frequent, unpleasant bouts of Montezuma's Revenge.

The "high-spirited romp" *Let's Go For Broke* was not only Duncan's first foray into the film industry – it was an opportunity to showcase Helm's talents on the big screen. Helm had previously worked on a horror film in 1972, *The Legacy of Satan*, but it wouldn't be released until 1976. In the meantime, Duncan's newest "spy spoof" was going to make her a star.

Helm, who had dreamed of stardom since childhood, was embracing every bit of her new life as a Hollywood diva. With designers, a make-up artist, and her own hair stylists and colorists,

Helm managed to increase the film's $700,000 budget to well over one million dollars.

Her role in *Let's Go For Broke* was that of "crusading reporter" Jackie Broke – described as "a cross between Barbara Walters and Barbarella," who somehow stumbles upon an international kidnapping conspiracy. Despite many of the other similar films from the early 1970's drawing on the "sexploitation" style, *Let's Go For Broke* maintained a PG rating – Helm refused to do any nude scenes, because she said her family was proud of her.

And not only did Duncan give Helm the opportunity to fill *Let's Go For Broke*'s lead role, he also allowed her to provide the vocals for the title song, which played during the film's credits.

Upon her return to New York, Helm fell back into her old habits – living the life of a disco-dancing party girl. Although she owned a lavish apartment in the city, Helm dated and even moved in with a number of famous suitors including New York Jets football superstar Joe Namath, assistant director Ron Walsh, and adult film producer Joseph (Jonas) Middleton.

With Middleton, Helm co-wrote her first film script – a grind-house film titled Illusions of a Lady that was released in 1974. Helm wasn't credited for her contributions to the project, and she and Middleton split up before the film's North American premiere. According to Helm, Middleton had "insisted" on shooting hardcore scenes for the triple X-rated film, which starred Andrea True and porn legend Jamie Gillis.

"He was shooting it hard," Helm said. "So I got in my car in my bikini and I drove home. He just sat there and let me carry out my own bags. I was livid."

The Hollywood life

Thanks to her popularity in New York, Helm had made a ton of connections in the film industry, and eventually decided to pursue her dream of Hollywood stardom with a move to California. She didn't give up on her party girl ways, though, and continued to hang out with famous musicians, actors, politicians, and even drug dealers.

Almost as soon as she arrived in Hollywood, Helm and her younger sister moved in with Bernard (Bernie) Cornfeld, an internationally renowned financier and insatiable womanizer. Not only did Cornfeld manage his banking, insurance, and mutual funds empire, he also ran a harem in his luxury Beverly Hills mansion. Grayhall Mansion, as it was known, had once belonged to the legendary silent film actor Douglas Fairbanks, Sr., but now housed centerfolds, starlets, and even call girls.

While Helm was certainly no stranger to using her womanly charms to get what she wanted from men and even help further her dream of Hollywood stardom, she was clear about what she would and wouldn't do to get ahead. According to columnist Earl Wilson, Helm had revealed that she'd been offered the chance to become a high-class call girl – but after some thought, Helm had declined the offer. Still, her lifestyle continued to verge on hedonistic.

"She lived as a free agent and frankly enjoyed sex," said a friend of Helm's.

One of Helm's oldest friends, Diane Mitchell, hadn't heard from Helm in over two years. In 1975, Mitchell received a call from her old friend, letting her know that she'd landed a few bit parts in Hollywood and had recently started dating actor Michael Sarrazin.

"It was a short conversation, no more than a few minutes," Mitchell admitted. "I got her telephone number and told her I would call her back. However, when I did call her back some time later, the phone had been disconnected. That was the last time I spoke with (Helm)."

In addition to Sarrazin, Helm continued flirtations with many more famous men – Warren Beatty, George Hamilton, Johnny Rivers, and Desi Arnaz, Jr – during her stay at Cornfeld's. The press also linked her with Englebert Humperdinck, Mick Jagger, and Roman Polansky.

"In the 70s, my mother knew a lot of people in Hollywood," said Helm's daughter, Nicole, who stayed with Helm occasionally in Los Angeles and would sometimes even attend parties with her. In fact, Nicole learned to swim in Humperdinck's famous heart-shaped pool.

"Whenever any male celebrities in town needed an escort, I was told they always thought of Mom first. She seemed to know everyone in town, and was very popular as the girl everyone wanted to be seen with."

Helm had also told friends at the time that she'd even been flown overseas to stay a week with the Shah of Iran. According to Nicole, the rumor was that the United States federal government would use models and starlets to glean information from foreign dignitaries.

"They apparently approached my mother to help them and she began filtering information to them on his activities," Nicole said. "The Shah was said to have given her many beautiful gifts, like jewelry and furs. I was told he was quite smitten with her but, you know, he had lots of other girls like Mom in his harem."

Although Helm was blessed with good looks, ambition, and the popularity to build many connections throughout the film industry, she was struggling to get her acting career off the ground. After her first two years in Los Angeles, she'd only earned herself a handful of gigs – a Coppertone television ad and appearances on two popular television shows. Helm played a roller-skating waitress on an episode of *Starsky and Hutch* in 1976, and for a memorable episode of *Wonder Woman* later that year, she took on a larger role as a beauty pageant contestant with attitude.

Her dream of being a Hollywood movie star still rested on her leading role in *Let's Go For Broke*, but the film production had stalled. Still, Helm continued to promote the film's release every chance she got, and was even rumored to have shot additional (and possibly more explicit) scenes for the now R-rated film.

Faced with life as a struggling actress, Helm decided to take advantage of the singing lessons she'd taken in New York. Thanks to her extensive networking with professionals in the music industry, Helm's desire to release a disco record could easily become a reality. New York DJ Frankie Crocker was brought in by Neil Bogart's Casablanca Records to work with Helm on the album, but Helm butted heads with her new producer.

The project introduced her to her next sexual conquest, though. Helm had begun exploring her "self-professed tendency" to bisexuality, and started seeing one of her backup singers, Patty Collins. Despite the fact that the two were said to be "inseparable," one of Helm's other backup singers, Debbie Danilow, said that Helm came on to her "immediately."

"She let me know she was interested in me (sexually) but wanted me to be comfortable with her first," Danilow said. "I more or less ignored her advances, all the time keeping my eye on Patty – who was keeping her eye on me ... But I accepted (Helm) as she was, and I appreciated her interest in me, even though it was not something we would act upon."

In fact, Danilow had met Helm on the night she was murdered. Although she hadn't gotten much opportunity to get to know Helm, Danilow still described her as "gifted and courageous, brilliant and creative, a rare shining light with no fear."

A night like any other

On February 12, 1977, Helm and her roommate were partying in Hollywood. It was a night like so many others, but would, sadly, come to a tragic and grisly end.

Helm had called a friend, a Hollywood talent scout named Sanford (Sandy) Smith, in an attempt to convince him to come out and join them at the party. When Smith declined, Helm decided to borrow her roommate's car and drive to Smith's house to talk him into it.

According to Smith, he'd been sleeping when she arrived, and he hadn't seen or heard her. It's possible she didn't even make it to the door. It's unclear if Helm was attacked on her way up to Smith's house or on her way back to the car.

Despite being a certified Black Belt, Helm couldn't get out of her assailant's grasp. After she was stabbed more than 30 times, including wounds to her face and neck, she was bludgeoned with a blunt object – possibly the handle of a knife, or maybe even a hammer. Her body was found fairly soon after the attack by a man crossing the street, who apparently discovered her with her roommate's car keys in her hand.

"I was told that my mother was lying partially under a parked car," Nicole said, "and that when he approached her, he heard her let out a long, deep breath – her last."

While Helm had made frequent appearances in the press and in gossip columns, there was surprisingly little coverage about her savage murder. One writer speculated that this may have been due to "who she knew and what she knew." This theory is supported by the fact that Helm's bag was missing – a bag that was thought to contain her "love diary," including valuable information that may have motivated her killer.

According to reports, this journal is said to contain all the names of Helm's famous lovers through the years – accompanied by detailed retellings of their most private moments. Her entanglements varied from industry professionals, actors and musicians, sports stars, and even political figures, like a town mayor who once gifted her with expensive jewelry.

Since Helm's murder more than three decades ago, police have interviewed more than 70 people – evidence collected into four notebooks full of names and pertinent information, and two boxes of investigative notes. DNA has since determined that her killer was a female, and due to the number of vital organs hit during the attack, it's speculated that it could have been the work of a professional contract killer.

The diary, which is said to be "potentially explosive," has never been recovered. Helm was also reported to have kept tapes of her sexual encounters, but these have also never been located. According to some sources, Helm planned to write a tell-all book detailing her history of liaisons with men, and was using the journal and the tapes to collect and preserve information for the book.

Many aspiring Hollywood starlets have fallen prey to the allure of a lifestyle of sex, drugs, money, and fame – but for Helm, this extravagant behaviour came at the ultimate price.

"Her beauty and charm were undeniable, and once she mastered the art of manipulation she found her way onto the path of her dreams," Nicole said. "My mother gained it all, and then lost it all in a very short time."

BOB CRANE : HOLLYWOOD'S UNSOLVED MURDER

JAIMI BENTON

Bob Crane, for anybody who doesn't know, was the actor who played Colonel Hogan in *Hogan's Heroes*. He reprised the role for six years, between 1965 and 1971.

Hogan's Heroes was Crane's first real taste of fame, but it was also his last. Though he toured the U.S. afterwards as part of a theater group, and starred in another sitcom, his career took a sharp downward turn after the cancellation of the show he was famous for.

But in a turn of events that turned his minor stardom to notoriety, Crane was murdered in 1978, in his own home. He was brutally beaten, maybe even strangled, in what seemed like a senseless attack. What made his death confusing was that there was no explanation for it-Crane was a family man, with no known enemies.

What came out of his case was a shock to the nation. Bob Crane, who was by all accounts a regular family man, had been living a debauched double life... One that could have led to his death.

Early Life

Crane was born in Connecticut, on July 13th, 1928. He was born in Waterbury, around the center of the state, but moved west to the border with New York State to live in Stamford as a child, and this is where he grew up.

From a young age, he showed an aptitude and affinity for music. He played drums in both junior high and high school, for the marching band. But following his graduation from high school, Crane chose not to go to college. Instead, he enlisted in the Connecticut Army National Guard, aged 20, and was given an honorable discharge two years later.

It was his enjoyment of music that led him into his first career: Crane began his career not as an actor, but as a radio host. His first shot at a broadcasting career was as a host for WLEA, a radio station in New York, not far from his Connecticut home in Stamford. He was hired in 1950. Around the same time, in 1949, Bob married his childhood sweetheart, Anne, and they settled down together.

His next jobs were in Bristol and in Bridgeport, working for WBIS (today WPRX) and WICC, Bridgeport's first radio station. By 1956, he had been noticed by CBS Radio, and he was flown out of the East Coast to host the morning show on KNX, the L.A. news radio station. As a radio show host, he received such notable names as Bob Hope, Frank Sinatra and Marilyn Monroe as guests.

Shot at Fame

Bob Crane's claim to fame was that he played Colonel Robert E. Hogan in WWII comedy *Hogan's Heroes*. He was offered the role in 1965.

The sitcom was based in a German P.O.W. camp, and starred Crane as the leader of a group of prisoners using the camp as a base for special operations. It was an instant hit, one of the top ten most viewed shows of the year according to ratings. With his experience drumming for his high school band, Crane even played the snare drum in the show's instantly recognisable introduction.

The show ran for six years, from 1965 to 1971, and can be considered a success. Crane was twice nominated for an Emmy Award, and Wener Klemperer (Colonel Klink) won twice. The show's best ratings came in the first 2 seasons, where it was number 9 and 17 in the ratings, respectively. It trailed out of the top thirty for the next four seasons, however, and so was cancelled. Despite being originally aired so long ago, the show still makes regular appearances on cable TV.

While the show was popular at the time, later critics have given it a hard time for making light of the real experiences of POWs, and trivializing German prison camps generally. But whatever our opinion of it today, the show was a success that lives on in popular culture.

After *Hogan's Heroes*

Following the cancellation of Hogan's Heroes, Crane struggled to find a way to revive his career. Rather than stick to just TV roles, he sought to broaden his experience with roles in films and on stage.

Around the same time, he also appeared in two lesser known Disney films: Superdad, produced in 1973, and Gus three years later. The first was a box office flop about a father (Crane) concocting a plot to prise his daughter away from her bad-influence friends. Paradoxically, Gus was a successful film about a football-playing mule. Crane did not take on the starring role (which would have certainly taken all of his acting skills), and it was his last ever film appearance.

One of his projects, the Bob Crane Show, seemed like it may have been the way back for Crane. The series was initially, aptly, named *Second Start*. The show hit the airwaves in 1975, four years, and was aired on NBC. Bob Crane's role- which was, of course, the starring role seeing as the show was named after him- was a step in a new direction for the actor. He played Bob Wilcox, a suburban family man who quits his day job to go to medical school.

But the series only lasted for 14 episodes, and was cancelled following very poor Nielsen ratings. This convinced Crane to stick with his theater production instead, *Beginner's Luck*, a play to which he had bought exclusive rights and began touring around the country. Bob, naturally, was both star and director. This seemed to satisfy him, and he toured it for five years, starting in 1973.

Murder

What stopped him wasn't a bad run, or poor reviews, but his own death. Crane was murdered at an apartment in suburban Scottsdale, on June 9th, 1978. He had been in the middle of a short run of his play, *Beginner's Luck*, at the local Windmill Dinner Theater.

He had been strangled with an electrical cord, which investigators discovered wrapped around his neck. The killer blow, however, had been dealt by a brutal blow to the skull. The actual weapon has never been identified, although investigators believe it to have been a camera tripod- indicating, perhaps, that Crane had been filming at the time.

He was buried around a month later, on July 9th, at St. Paul the Apostle Catholic Church in L.A, mourned by several hundred attendees.

The first suspect was Crane's friend, John Henry Carpenter. He was Crane's right hand man, some would say his best friend. But he was spotted in Scottsdale on the day of Crane's death, and was seen by two hotel desk clerks visiting Crane in his room. They recalled that after he left that morning, he appeared nervous while waiting for his cab to the airport.

There were nowhere near enough clues to work with, however, in order to bring about a prosecution. Prosecutors refused to go forward with the case, and so Carpenter wasn't forced to stand trial.

What kind of a man was Bob Crane?

Bob Crane had been well regarded by his friends, family and fans. An ABC News report, written after his death, described him as "the ideal leading man — handsome, clean-cut, [and] likable," and they weren't far off the mark.

Robert Clary, the man who played French POW Louis LeBeau in *Hogan's Heroes,* recalled that "Bob was a very charming man. He was easy to get along with — he never acted like, 'I'm making much more money than you do, and you better listen to what I'm saying.' That was wonderful."

Karen Crane, Bob's daughter, had similar fond memories of her father. "My dad was an absolute typical family man at home," she recalled. "He was always swimming with us, playing with us. I just have wonderful memories of my dad and my years growing up."

But what shocked the public just as much as Crane's senseless murder, were the revelations that came out about his life shortly afterwards- revelations that destroyed Crane's pleasant image.

Image and Reality

What his family and the fans from his *Hogan's Heroes* years didn't know was that Bob Crane wasn't a wholesome man..

Way back in 1993, the *Phoenix New Times* released an incredible transcript of a conversation between Crane and his friend, Carpenter. In the tape, the pair discuss their favourite ways of striking lucky with women. Both Crane and Carpenter were described as "alley cats who tried their luck with almost anything female that came their way" by the *Phoenix Sun Times*, which luridly detailed their sexual exploits.

The pair made good friends: because of Carpenter's social contacts, Crane was provided "with a ready supply of willing women that surely wouldn't have been otherwise available to him", and due to Carpenter's expertise in video recording, the pair found an outlet for their desires.

But Crane's pleasures were unusual, far further beyond normal infidelity. Mark Dawson, son of Crane's co-star of *Hogan's Heroes* Richard Dawson, detailed how one day shortly after turning 17 he was introduced to Crane's hidden life.

"He was carting a couple of videotapes and a Polaroid book," Dawson said in an interview to ABC, years after Crane's death. "He went into the other room and then called me in: 'Hey, come on in ... you want to take a look at this stuff?'" Dawson had no idea what he was coming to see. It was a sordid collection of pornographic movies and photographs- all of them starring Bob Crane himself.

Mark Dawson's connection was through his father, who had initially introduced Crane and Carpenter.

"The first 10 or 15 minutes, it was very interesting. Unnerving. I gotta tell you: it was a little shocking to see Colonel Hogan au naturel. Couldn't watch Hogan's the same way again after that," Dawson recalled.

Crane was not just excited, but almost took pride in showing off his collection. "It was like wow, look at this one, look at that one. I don't know if 'proud' is the right word but sort of 'look what I got. She's a real winner, huh?' Some of them pwere, and some of them weren't. He was excited, he was happy about it. He was like a kid with a toy."

Affairs

Aside from the one night stands, Crane had also had regular affairs with his co-actors in *Hogan's Heroes*, and introduced them to his hobby.

He began an affair with Cynthia Lynn, not behind closed doors, but actually on set. During one scene, the pair had been called on by the story to kiss: "We're kissing," Cynthia said to ABC, "and they say "Cut!" And we're still kissing." This was in 1965, while Crane was still married to his childhood sweetheart.

But that was far from the last of their affair. "He was a camera nut, OK? I loved it when he took pictures of me, because he was like a kid in a candy store. Yes, he took some nude pictures of me. But it was nothing to be ashamed of. There was nothing kinky or weird or about it," she told reporters.

Cynthia left the show after just one season, but Crane didn't find it difficult to move on. Patricia Annette Olson, better known as Sigrid Valdis, was the next woman seduced by Crane. "He was always hitting on me from day one- but he would hit on any bimbo that would walk on that set. It didn't matter. I mean, that was just Bob," she told ABC. They quickly began an affair.

A Strained Relationship?

But in what might be one of the strangest revelations of all, Bob's wife Pat Crane spoke to ABC about his affairs, how she knew all along- and how she didn't mind at all. It was many years later, and the first time that she had ever opened up about the case or about Bob's affairs.

"He didn't lose his first amendment rights when he married me — he loved having sex and filming it," she told the interviewer. "He never broke any laws. Nothing he did was unconstitutional. From almost the first day on the set, he told me his hobby was photography — I didn't figure it was landscape! He brought over a double-thick briefcase, and it was filled with like four rows of slides in a box about that big. So there were thousands of slides in there ... of all the women in his life."

And even though she knew of his affairs, she said that it didn't hurt her feelings. "No... I know it sounds crazy. Maybe people listening to me will think I am crazy! Bob used these women. He said, 'I wish when I finished with them I could just push a button and they'd fall through the floor and disappear.' Now, how could I be jealous of something like that? He treated women like the rest of the world treats toilet paper. Who's going to be jealous of toilet paper?"

"They were using each other. Everybody was getting what they wanted out of this. And it wasn't anybody's business but theirs. I knew he wouldn't [stop]. I knew that ... he ... he had had this obsession, he couldn't help it, there was nothing for me to be jealous of."

Bob didn't even try to keep it a secret, which may be surprising to some people. Their relationship functioned normally even though he was having sex with other women. "No, he'd usually call me up and tell me what he'd just done, or how he'd done it. I wanted the openness, I just didn't want to participate."

And no, their relationship was not strained. "Yes, we were happy together. We had a wonderful sex life. We had a wonderful marriage." It never came close to being public knowledge, and wasn't even revealed to friends or family: "No one knew."

Investigation

The investigation was led by the Scottsdale Police Department. But unfortunately for Crane, their small size meant that they didn't even have a homicide department that could work on the case. The scene also didn't yield any clues that might have identified some of the more traditional reasons for a murder: nothing of value had been stolen from Crane's apartment that morning, and nobody had forced their way in through the door or window. It clearly wasn't going to be as simple as that; the investigators would have to look elsewhere for clues.

Those clues came in the form of Crane's collection of recordings, the same collection that Mark Dawson described. A number of the tapes featured Carpenter, who had visited Crane that day: naturally, he became the primary person of interest in the case.

Carpenter's rental car was investigated immediately, and blood smears were found in it- crucially, matching Crane's blood type. Of course, DNA testing wasn't available in 1978, and so that was the only evidence tying Carpenter to the murder. Prosecutors refused to press on with the case due to the lack of any evidence apart from this; and with that, the case went dead.

Carpenter remained a free man, and nobody else could be identified as a suspect. Police did believe that Crane may have been killed in a film gone wrong, but there was no way of finding any leads if that was the case.

Reopening of the case

For twelve years, the case stayed cold. But in 1990, after a new county attorney started a push to finally make some breakthroughs on cold murder cases, there was a new determination to finally catch Crane's killer.

And why not? The investigators still had the blood samples discovered in Carpenter's car, as well as photographic evidence. While Crane's death remained a mystery, it seemed as if prosecutors would be able to make a case- especially with a recently re-discovered piece of evidence, found by Jim Raines, Scottsdale detective.

The key evidence was not a physical exhibit- it was a photograph, of what was supposed to have been a speck of body tissue inside Carpenter's rental car. Similar evidence had been found around Crane's bed. Experts said that it was fat tissue, but since the car had been cleaned since, it was impossible to say.

Fat tissue is a common form of residue after brutal assault, and the idea was that the tiny piece of tissue had stuck to the murder weapon as Carpenter made his way away from the scene.

While the tissue samples from inside Crane's apartment had been preserved, those found in Carpenter's rental car had been lost since the initial investigation. The photograph therefore became a key talking point for both the prosecution and defence. But this was considered enough for the case to go to trial.

While Crane's family were happy that the killer might finally be identified- in particular Bob Crane's son, who has always suspected Carpenter- there were others who sprang to his defence. Mark Dawson for instance, Richard Dawson's son, had become a documentary filmmaker since the days that he was first introduced to Crane's world. He and Carpenter remained friends throughout the years, and he came out on Carpenter's side.

"He's in the jam of his life, and it's time to pay him back a little for his friendship," Dawson said to the *Phoenix New Times*. "I have never seen anything of the side of him that Arizona is trying to portray—this murderous monster." But whether Carpenter was a murderous monster, and whether he truly was Crane's killer, could finally be decided in a court of law- twelve years after Bob's untimely death, at the age of just 49.

Carpenter's day in court

It took until 1992 for John Carpenter to stand trial for Crane's murder. Carpenter had been Crane's friend for over a decade, and because of both this and the lurid details that came out in the trial, the case was a news reporter's dream. While some details of Crane's second life had come out after the discovery of his body, the trial reinvigorated interest in the second life of the former *Hogan's Heroes* star, and the case was therefore featured heavily on major news networks.

Carpenter was accused of having bludgeoned Crane to death, over a threat that the actor would cut him out of his life- and out of the ready supply of women that he gave Carpenter access to. The Maricopa County deputy attorney, Bob Shutts, accused Carpenter of having "fed off the energy and fame of the actor", and that "Bob Crane became a source of women that he could never obtain for himself". This was Carpenter's supposed motive, and the central argument of the prosecution.

Indeed, it came out during the trial that Crane had "complained to friends and his son that he was getting irritated with Carpenter, and told one woman he and his friend were 'on the outs'", according to the Pittsburgh Post-Gazette. There were even insinuations that Carpenter had been in love with Crane, which could potentially have explained his violent outburst.

Carpenter gave an extensive interview to the *Phoenix New Times* during the case, in which he was adamant on the topic of his innocence. "I don't go around and kill my pals... I played around a lot, balled a lot of women, and I've made mistakes that hurt people close to me. I'm no saint."

"But I never even had a fight with Bob, goddammit. He was my friend. And he was the goose who laid the golden egg for me, in terms of meeting ladies."

Carpenter's defence attorney, Stephen Avilla, expected that his client would be acquitted. The defence based their case on the lack of substantial physical evidence, as well as the lack of a strong motive. While the prosecution did argue that Carpenter had been angered by Crane's decision to cut him out of his life, this evidence was circumstantial and far from definitive.

Moreover, the DNA testing of the blood had come back inconclusive, and couldn't be linked to either Carpenter or Crane with any certainty, despite the unlikelihood of it having come from anybody else. There was also the small fact of the murder weapon never having been found, despite having been surmised to be a camera tripod. All in all, the defence argued that the evidence available just wasn't enough.

And they were right. Carpenter was found not guilty: what little evidence the prosecution could point to couldn't be sufficient to take away John's freedom, no matter what had been speculated. Carpenter, quite naturally, maintained his innocence and claimed the victory; the prosecution could do little but complain of how the case had been mishandled from the start.

No matter the reason why, however, John Carpenter remained a free man.

Auto Focus (Movie)

Although the case had been settled by law, the mystery of Bob's death remained, and so did interest in the sordid details of his murder. In 2002, the entire affair was dramatized in the movie *Auto Focus,* starring Willem Dafoe and Greg Kinnear.

At the time, Kinnear and Joe Schrader, the director, gave interviews on why they found Crane's story so interesting. "What's fascinating about him is this sort of contradictory nature," Kinnear told ABC. "I mean, he really saw himself as a one-woman man! And yet there were reams and reams of photographs and video of all these other behaviors going on."

Paul Schrader added: "He really did live that classic life of the hypocritical Hollywood star... He portrayed himself as a conservative Republican family man." This classic story, coupled with the mystery surrounding the murder, showed how the case could still capture the American imagination- although it was unclear what else could be done to solve it.

The movie dramatized Crane's story, especially in terms of highlighting his supposedly 'hypocritical' life. Scotty Crane criticised *Auto Focus* after its release: Paul Schrader had portrayed Bob as a church-going man who claimed to live a moral life, which Scotty claimed couldn't be further from the truth, as his father almost never went to church.

Despite these inconsistencies, Roger Ebert described the movie as "brilliant" and gave it a glowing review.

Mark Dawson served as technical advisor to the film, to give the producers valuable insight into the real life exploits of Crane and Carpenter. He has also been working on a documentary about the pair and their lives, although it is unclear when this might be coming out.

2016 DNA Testing

Just in the last year, however, a new development was made in Crane's case- even though it was 38 years since his death. Because of advancements in the field of DNA testing since the original case, it was now possible to analyse the small, but significant, amounts of blood found on the door of Carpenter's rental car.

The results were revealed to a panel, members of whom included the prosecutor of the original case, Carpenter's lawyer, and Bob Crane Jr. John Hook- the Fox News reporter who had the DNA samples retested- stated that "the DNA found on the door of John Carpenter's rental car is not... from Bob Crane."

The DNA was, in fact, two different profiles. One was from a man, whose identity remains unknown; the other "is a partial profile too degraded to reach any conclusions," the Fox reporter stated during the big reveal.

Crane Jr. was clearly surprised by the results, mouthing "wow" as Hook read them out. He later said to the press, "I'm shocked right now... There were always two people in my mind: John Carpenter and my stepmother, for different reasons. But it was on John's car."

Crane Jr. had suspected Carpenter for obvious reasons. But he had also suspected his stepmother because of the case of Bob's will: nothing had been left to any of his children, or to his ex-wife. Every cent had been left to Patricia Olson.

Carpenter's lawyer also spoke after the results came out. "This is wonderful news for his family," Avilla said. "This is wonderful news for John who has passed away to know that he has finally been vindicated... Not only in a court of law, but in a court of public opinion."

Case closed?

The mystery of Bob Crane's murder is never likely to be solved.

It's impossible to say where the case can go from here. The evidence has been turned over time and time again; the photograph, the blood, the DNA. Nothing has definitively led to an answer of who murdered Bob Crane, let alone why.

Besides, it was only four years after the verdict of the court case that John Carpenter died, of a heart attack. So even if he could have finally been tied to Crane's murder by DNA evidence, justice could never have been done.